BEYOND *the* BARRIERS

Overcoming Hard Times Through Tough Faith

HAROLD MORRIS
Author of *Twice Pardoned*

PUBLISHING

Pomona, California

BEYOND THE BARRIERS: Overcoming Hard Times Through Tough Faith
Copyright © 1987 by Harold Morris

The names and descriptions of many people in this book
have been changed to protect their identities.

Library of Congress Cataloging-in-Publication Data

Morris, Harold.
Beyond the barriers.

    1. Christian life—1960-   . 2. Morris, Harold.
    I. Title.
BV4501.2.M587   1987   248.4   87-82302
ISBN 0-84-9999-93-6

Published by Focus on the Family Publishing, Pomona, California 91799.
Distributed by Word Books, Waco, Texas.

Printed in the United States of America
87 88 89 90 91 92 / 10 9 8 7 6 5 4 3 2 1

To three dear friends and fellow servants
of our Lord and Savior, Jesus Christ:
Bobby Richardson,
Bob Norris, and
Edwin Tucker
These men have stood in the gap with me
through all the heartache and hard times;
taught me that it takes preparation before performance; and
helped me realize that regardless of the circumstance,
we all share alike and will be judged
according to our faithfulness to God.
To them, I say thank you
for helping make this book possible,
for believing in me, discipling me,
and teaching me the true meaning
of tough faith.

CONTENTS

ACKNOWLEDGMENTS

I would like to thank Al Janssen for his help with this book.

I would also like to express my appreciation to Rick Christian for his assistance. But most of all I'd like to thank him for believing in me, for his encouragement, and for his friendship. Without him this book would not have been possible.

INTRODUCTION

The words of the judge still ring in my memory. "Young man, for the crime of armed robbery, I sentence you to hard labor at the state penitentiary for the rest of your natural life. And for the crime of murder, I sentence you to hard labor at the state penitentiary for the rest of your natural life." Even now I remember his face as he turned to the bailiffs and ordered, "Take him away."

The night of my conviction was one of the loneliest of my life. As I lay in my cell, the finality of the verdict began to soak in. Over and over I heard the words of the jury: *Guilty as charged! Guilty as charged! Guilty! Guilty! Guilty!*

Though I was eventually paroled and pardoned of these charges, nothing will ever erase from my mind the nine-and-a-half years of fear that haunted me night and day while locked up with psychotic killers, rapists, robbers, thugs, and thieves. At Georgia State Penitentiary I witnessed dozens of murders and scores of stabbings and mutilations. My life was threatened repeatedly, and many times those threats were more than mere words. As I fell asleep each night I wondered if it would be my last. I could be stabbed for no reason other than the way I looked, the color of my skin, or for the warm Pepsi Colas in my cell. My life was also in danger because I'd become a Christian. On a sliding scale, talking with God was on par with ratting to the warden. In the state penitentiary, you'd be persecuted for doing either.

As an ex-convict who served nine-and-a-half years of a double-life sentence for crimes I didn't commit, I began my Christian walk under trying circumstances to say the least. I learned early that the rewards of discipleship don't come without struggle and effort. When I finally attained my freedom from prison, I learned that I didn't leave those hardships behind bars. Satan found new ways to fight me, to tempt me, to discourage me. I now wake up in my own home in my own room in my own bed, without battling the fear of attacks from other convicts. Yet I struggle today with a far more lethal adversary: cancer. The cells in my body have rebelled, and hold my body hostage. Once again, there are many nights when I close my eyes, unsure how much longer I will live.

Convicts and cancer. I pray that those reading this book will never have to deal with either. But we share other adversaries which are the result of a fallen world. Sorrow, tragedy, heartache, insecurity, and loneliness belong to us all. Financial hardships, broken promises, disintegrating friendships, shattered dreams— they hound us daily. These are just a few of the hurdles we must overcome if we are to finish the race as victorious Christians. Because our faith is always under attack, I am convinced that the most difficult thing anybody anywhere will ever attempt is to fulfill a Christian life. Only Christ could live it perfectly.

Though difficult, it's the most meaningful, purposeful, and rewarding life anybody could live. Living the Christian life is the absolute, number one, most important thing anybody will ever do. That's the reason I wrote my first book, *Twice Pardoned*, which details my rags-to-roaches life story. And that's also the reason I've written this book, *Beyond the Barriers*. In my Christian life, I've probably had more struggles than most people . . . and have the scars to prove it! Yet along the way I've learned that overcoming hard times is only possible with tough faith. Not a Sunday school faith, but a hard, gutsy, fighting faith. And this book is my best effort to describe for you exactly what that kind of tough faith involves . . . and exactly how and why, as ex-con #62345, I keep trusting Jesus, even though "keeping the faith" has sometimes been hazardous to my health.

I want to accomplish several purposes in this book. First, I want to *ponder the past*. I can't forget where I've come from or what God has done for me. I can't forget His grace, His forgiveness, His love. Even as I was surrounded by hardened convicts, I knew God was with me. I had faith. When I developed extensive cancer—just after my miraculous pardon and things had begun to look up—even then I felt God's hand of blessing.

Second, I'd like to *proclaim the present.* Just as important as what I've been saved from is what I've been saved for. It's a tremendous joy to see God unfold the purpose of my salvation day by day. There was a time when all I cared about was to save my own neck and make it through the night alive. So you can imagine my feelings to see God use my life to save others— particularly other prisoners and young people—for eternity. There was a time when I thought my life wasn't worth much. But now that I know I have supreme, eternal value to God, I can face each new day as a one-of-a-kind adventure. Faith makes it possible.

Finally, I'd like to *project the future.* I don't pretend to have special abilities to see beyond today. Yet the way God has worked in my life in the past, coupled with the way I see His hand in my life now, I have faith that there is good ahead. For that reason, I've tried to invest my life in the most important goal there is: to mirror Jesus Christ in my life. Though I'm just an ex-con, I'm no dummy. I'm smart enough to know that life without Christ is really no life at all.

Faith links each stage of my life (and each chapter of the book) together. Contrary to what you sometimes hear on TV, being a Christian is no cakewalk. And if your Christianity is going to matter, your faith must be tough. Tough enough to withstand hard times and heartache, suffering and affliction. In Philippians 1:12, Paul was referring to his imprisonment, beatings and suffering when he wrote: "Now I want you to know, brothers, that what has happened to me has really served to advance the gospel." These could actually be my words. Even when bad things happen to God's people, He uses the circumstances to help them understand there is a God. In other words, when we think *bad*, God thinks *good*.

I'll be honest, though. I've felt like quitting on God many times. When my fellow prisoners, the guards, and even the parole board wrote off my Christian conversion as being some kind of con game and kept insisting I'd die in prison—sure, I felt like giving up. But I didn't. When doctors said nothing more could be done for my cancer and told me not to get involved in any serious relationship because I probably wouldn't make it—sure, I felt ready to call it quits. But I didn't. Rather, I toughed out the low times in blind faith to my unseen Lord. I'd just get on my knees and ask God to give me the strength I needed for that moment. Not for the whole day, but just for that very moment. And He gave me staying power when I hung in there like that and kept believing. He did with me, and He will with you. I didn't have all the answers, but I kept believing. I had my doubts, but I kept believing.

That's tough faith. On the following pages, I want to show you how it works.

Harold Morris

Chapter One

MEMORIES

The broiling summer sun glinted off rows of chain link fence, topped with barbed wire and blanketed with coils of razor wire. It was a menacing barrier—seemingly capable of tearing and slicing anyone who even dared to look at it. And for good reason: Behind it rose an imposing cement structure, home to one thousand of the world's most violent men: murderers, robbers, and rapists with spine-chilling nicknames such as Phantom, Shotgun Kelly, Big Mac, Latcheye, Railroad, Scar Face, Big Money, Mad Dog, Monkey Man, and Lug Wrench.

Six towers, each manned by a rifle-toting guard, loomed above this fortress, otherwise known as Georgia State Penitentiary. Occasionally an inmate would challenge the odds and attempt an escape. If the fence didn't stop him, the ever-vigilant patrols would pump him full of lead. For a fleeting moment as I stood in the shadows of the prison, I thought of Bull Jackson, who caught a bullet while trying to vault the fence on a rainy Georgia night.

For those very few who might, through some ingenious plan or incredible happenstance, penetrate these initial lines of defense, the surrounding countryside formed another barrier. In three directions lay ten thousand acres of open farmland that produced food for most of Georgia's prison population. The fields provided easy hunting ground for posses and their bloodhounds. The only other escape route was into a serene looking forest that hid a swamp populated by man-eating mosquitoes, snakes, and

alligators. Men who entered that jungle inevitably surrendered—
willing to return to prison after two or three miserable days experiencing the worst Mother Nature had to offer.

As I surveyed the knife-like fencing before me and the pastoral
scenery behind me, memories of my years on the wrong side of
life flooded my mind. Despite the unbearably hot and muggy
weather, I shivered as I recalled my first view of this setting.
Shackled in handcuffs and leg irons, I was transferred to Georgia
State Penitentiary in 1971 after two and one-half years in Fulton
County Jail. As I stood at the gate a guard instructed me to take
one final look over my shoulder. "You will die here," he snarled.
"You will never be free again."

Against all odds, I walked through the gate to freedom seven
years later. So why was I now drawn back to this desolate prison?
Certainly not to admire the picturesque landscape. And definitely
not for a slug of nostalgia, because this had been the scene of
innumerable nightmares. Here a man had beaten me over the
head till I nearly died. Here I'd seen two men gouge the eyes
out of an inmate on a bunk eighteen inches from mine. Here I'd
seen men die by murder and suicide, their bodies carted past my
cell.

But this was also the place of my greatest triumph, the day
when I knelt in my roach-infested cell and prayed, trusting Christ
for the forgiveness of my sins. Here, God had started a super-
natural transformation of my life.

Fifty-five times in the first two and one-half years following
my parole, I'd returned to this site to speak at chapel services
and crusades, to visit old friends in their cells and offer them an
alternative to their hopeless existence. Then for several years the
authorities banned all visitors in order to totally refurbish the
institution.

The renovation was certainly overdue. Originally built for 750
men, the prison population had swelled to 3,200 by the time of
my release. I'd seen as many as seventeen men crammed inside
an eight-by-ten-foot cell. Violence and murder were a way of
life. Drugs flowed like water into the institution. Riots were
ignited over real and perceived injustices. Racial tension was

always present and hung in the air like summer humidity. Health and cleanliness were virtually impossible due to the filth of plugged up toilets, and the disease-carrying insects and rodents which freely roamed every inch of the prison. Simply put, the penitentiary was a place you wouldn't want a dog to live, if you cared about dogs.

During the reform era, the government spent millions of dollars to upgrade the main building, construct individual cells, improve medical facilities, and install surveillance cameras. Most of the inmates had been shipped to other prisons, and now only the one thousand most dangerous criminals remained.

With all of the changes complete, it was still an awful place. After several requests, the warden finally permitted me to again visit the men in their cells.

Stepping through the doors of the prison vestibule, I stated my intended business to a uniformed woman, who was shielded from me by an inch-thick pane of bulletproof glass. On this visit, I was accompanied by Chip Murray, an Atlanta banker, and two other friends. Without a twitch of a smile, the guard took our drivers' licenses and phoned the main office. She nodded curtly, and then punched a button to release an electronically-controlled, steel door. We passed through a narrow walkway, lined with the ever-present razor wire, and entered the main prison building, a giant block of concrete that had withstood the elements and untold coats of paint since its construction in 1936. It looked like a low-budget city hall, minus the manicured lawn and statues.

Inside the rotunda, I asked for a cup of water to soothe my throat, which was constantly dry because cancer-killing radiation treatments had also burned away my saliva glands.

"Super Honky!" one of the guards suddenly yelled, "how are you doing?" It had been years since I'd heard that nickname, bestowed by black inmates because of my athletic prowess. "You haven't changed a bit," the guard said, as he stood there smiling.

"Got better looking," I responded.

The guard laughed, took our drivers' licenses, stamped our wrists with a light-sensitive ink and then had us step through a metal detector. Next, he summoned the deputy warden, Darren

Fields, who welcomed us to the institution and offered to give us a tour before we began visiting inmates in their cells. We accepted the invitation and followed him through a thick steel door, which slammed on our heels. The clang of metal on metal sounded like a collision of two diesel train engines and reverberated in my head even after the noise had died in the cement hallway.

The other sounds of prison were equally harsh. There was constant yelling and swearing, rattling of cell doors, and the clanging of utensils and pots in the mess hall. And then there were the bells. As they rang, I recalled how they had ruled my life for so many years. They woke us up, called us to meals, and ordered lights out. Every two hours the bell blasted to signal the time for inmates to be counted, and then sounded again when guards had accounted for all the men.

There were more clanging doors to pass through, and with each it seemed like I was descending deeper into hell. A repulsive odor, worse than a crowded locker room after a big game, invaded my nostrils. I'd forgotten how bad a prison could smell. In the free world, people bathe daily, use deodorant, wash sheets and clothes, and flush toilets. When I was in prison, most inmates seldom used deodorant, rarely bathed, changed sheets and underwear once a week, if that, and intentionally plugged up toilets for entertainment.

I was also struck by the absence of color. I'd forgotten how plain my world had been without bright shades of red, blue, orange, and purple. The prison walls were painted a drab green to cover previous coats of drab brown, drab yellow, and drab ivory. The concrete floors were unpainted. And not even the government's millions of dollars in renovation could correct the depressing sight.

Our first tour stop was the morgue. At one end of the room, rising off the floor like an altar, stood a large stainless steel table upon which autopsies were performed. As I surveyed the room and bright lights and cadaver drawers, I thought back to my first year in the penitentiary. I'd been assigned to clerk for the doctor, and one day reported for work to the morgue. There I saw a black man stretched out on a table with his arm raised in the air. "What you doin'?" I asked. "Taking five?" It seemed a strange place to nap, but then there weren't many quiet spots where a man could catch a few minutes of peace.

When the man didn't answer, I asked what was wrong with his arm. Again he didn't respond, so I repeated the question. When he still didn't speak, I turned to the guard by the door. "What's with this guy? He doesn't want to talk."

"By God, I guess he doesn't!" the guard said with a laugh. "He was stabbed all to pieces."

I thought he was joking. But when I stepped around the table, I saw the man's guts were lying in front of him, his knee was sliced up, and the muscles had been cut out of his arm. Evidently he'd thrown up his arm to defend himself against attack, and rigor mortis had frozen his body in this pose of death. It was my job to take pictures of the body and measure the wounds for the doctor, who in turn wrote up a formal report. I counted fourteen stab wounds in his chest, any one of which, the doctor told me, could have killed him.

I was told that after I saw a few bodies I would become callous. Maybe death didn't bother most inmates because it was so "everyday," and because life had little value in prison. But I never became desensitized to such butchery. Even all of these years later, I couldn't rid my mind of the men whose bloody corpses had lain on this shiny table.

The next step was Death Row, where I'd spent six of the worst months of my life. As we walked down the dimly lit corridor, I could still hear the words of Shotgun Kelly growling in the cell beside mine, "Hey, next door. If I get out of this cell, I'm going to kill you!" That was my welcome.

I stepped into a little holding room beside the electric chair where condemned men had spent their final minutes on earth. I looked up at a small bar-covered window cut high in the wall, through which inmates got their last look at the sky before they were executed. Some unexplainable emotion gripped me, and I felt tears cloud my eyes. A total of 484 men had stood in this same spot, looking up for their last view of this world, and most of them died without any hope.

That's what bothered me. And that's what drew me back to the penitentiary. Just a few cells away, in 1973, I'd lived here without hope. One day a man visited my cell and tried to tell me about the love of Jesus. My response was to take some filthy water from the commode and throw it in his face. Now as I looked through the barred window at the deep blue sky, I thanked God for the incredible distance Jesus Christ had put between me and those days on death row. If only I could help another hopeless man realize that his sins could be forgiven, and his guilt removed. If only I could give him a taste of heaven while confined in this earthly hell.

As the deputy continued the tour, I wondered how I would be received by the inmates after so many years. Many of my old buddies would be gone, either paroled or transferred. Some, like Bull Jackson, were no doubt dead. A few might recognize me, but that didn't mean I would be welcomed. Inmates had a strong "us versus them" mentality, and I was now a "them." I represented something they might never attain and preferred not to talk about, freedom. Once you'd been released, it didn't take them long to forget you. Misery loves company, and I was guilty of having deserted their world. I'd become an outsider. I could visit; they had to live here.

On March 14, 1978, I left Georgia State Penitentiary on parole. Three years later, the governor of Georgia issued me a total pardon, wiping out all record of my crimes and restoring my rights as a citizen of the United States. Nevertheless, no one could take the prison out of Harold Morris.

The undeniable fact was that this penitentiary remained part of my everyday life. It affected the way I talked, the way I hurt, the way I loved. I'd seen men bleed from the inside out because nobody cared for them. Knowing they were desperate for love, and remembering the years when no one loved me, I often went overboard to express love to people. It also affected how I dealt with perceived injustice. Instinctively, I could back someone into a corner if I believed I was right. Sometimes I forced people to face unpleasant facts that they didn't want to face.

But the underlying factor, the one that drove me back into prison, was the fact that God had reached through the bars of a filthy, roach-infested cell in this very prison and touched my life. On February 19, 1974, I'd taken the first step of faith and started on an incredible spiritual journey. Over the years as my faith grew, it seemed natural to tell other inmates about my Lord and Savior.

The deputy interrupted my thoughts by asking me if I remembered Bull Jackson. I stopped and looked at him funny.

"Sure," I answered. "He was the meanest con I ever knew. I remember when he was killed in an escape attempt."

"Shot, but not killed," he said. "He survived, and is still here."

I stopped in my tracks. "Then I'd like to see him," I said.

The guard shook his head. "That may not be possible. Nobody has to tell you about ol' Bull. He's the most dangerous man here, and anything could set him off."

As we resumed our walk, I couldn't help thinking about the fear Bull instilled in inmates and guards alike while I was in prison. I'd seen him smash a man's head with a bedrail—just because the guy accidentally bumped his bed. He hated blacks, and he'd attack them at any time, without reason.

Somehow I managed to get on his bad side. At the time I was overseeing the athletic teams and supplies. Bull wanted to run the boxing team, and he stuck his nose in my face every day trying to get me to give him that job. He called me every name in the book, threatened my mother with great bodily harm, and let it be known that he wouldn't mind if I was discovered in the athletic shed with a baseball bat wrapped around my skull. He was pretty persuasive, but I wasn't as dumb as I looked. Bull never lost a fight, and I wasn't ready to die. So whenever he approached me, I simply walked away. He eventually found someone else he wanted to kill more than me, and things cooled down.

"How about letting me see Bull, even for just a few minutes," I asked again.

"We can't let him out of the cell," the deputy said. "He'll kill somebody or start a riot. All the inmates, even the guards, are scared of him."

It sounded as if nothing had changed. He was a man who'd find a way to kill with his fist, a board, a spoon, possibly even a Q-tip, without batting an eye. I'd met many killers in prison. Deep inside, most of them had cowardly personalities. You could go to sleep at night with them around and not worry too much. But Bull was pure killer, and you didn't dare close your eyes when he was awake.

"You don't have to let him out. Just let me talk to him through his cell door."

"I don't know. I think it would be better if you didn't."

"It's very important," I persisted.

"I'll check with the warden," he said, stopping by one of the guard stations to use the phone.

As I waited, I wondered about my persistence. Why should I force myself to see a man no one cared about? Who would criticize me for letting this opportunity pass? It seemed like I was constantly putting myself in the toughest situations to witness for Christ.

I thought about my first witness inside these walls—to a homosexual. I'd always despised homosexuals, yet they were an undeniable element of prison life. During one of my first days in prison, long before I'd become a Christian, a guard had pointed at a bald-headed man standing against the wall and asked me to summon him. So I walked over, tapped him on the shoulder, and said, "Sir, the officer would like to see you."

The man spun around, and I discovered that his eyebrows were plucked and his ears pierced. "How dare you address me as Sir," he chided in an unnaturally high voice, placing his hands on his hips. "My name is Roberta, and you will address me as such, or never speak to me again."

The guard nearly died laughing, as did the other inmates nearby. I was so mad that I returned a few minutes later, ready to rearrange Roberta's face. "Hey, fag!" I growled. "How'd you like a roll in the hay?" By being derogatory, I thought I could prompt a fight. I had my fist balled up, and was ready to knock his teeth out for humiliating me.

"A roll in the hay?" he sang out. "Honey, together we'll light the hay on fire."

I was shocked. I had expected him to challenge me. Instead, he flaunted his homosexuality. He was proud of it. I soon discovered that probably three out of four inmates participated in homosexual behavior. Thus, I had to learn to tolerate them even though I could not accept their behavior. To survive in prison, I couldn't look down at anybody. I couldn't think I was better than anybody else. So I adopted a philosophy of *I'll be good to you, if you're good to me*. That changed after I became a Christian. With Christ's help, my philosophy became, *I'll be good to you even if you're not good to me*.

When I decided to witness to a homosexual, I targeted a guy called Peaches, a name derived from the fact that others thought he was so sweet. He was tall and skinny, with a light, milk chocolate complexion. He plucked his eyebrows into a high arch, wore a stud earring, and dressed in clothes starched stiff as cardboard. He was immaculate, with every hair neatly combed.

One day I found him outside, standing by himself. I'd just spent time reading my Bible and was feeling pretty cocky and spiritual. I didn't know exactly where to begin, so I just said, "Hey, Peaches, you need Jesus."

"Is that right, big boy?" he smirked.

"Yeah, Jesus will take care of you; He'll straighten out your life."

His eyes were cold, but amused. He winked at me.

"You need to be born again," I continued. "You need Christ in your life. Jesus died for you, you know."

"Yeah? Show me," he said. "You've got your little Bible there with you. Show me where He died for me."

I opened my New Testament, but didn't know where it talked about Jesus' death on the cross. I stood there flipping pages, hoping that somehow the Bible would miraculously fall open to the right page. It didn't. The more frustrated I became, the bigger Peaches' smile grew.

"Well?" he asked.

"I can't find it, but I know He died for you."

"Right. And you got any idea what being born again even means?"

There was an awkward silence. I didn't know how to explain that, either. I knew Jesus died for him, but he wanted to see it in black and white. He wanted the Word of God, not the word of a man with a double-life sentence. I was a nobody.

"Let me see your little Bible," Peaches suddenly said. I handed it to him, and he promptly turned to Romans 5:8 and read, "But God demonstrated his own love for us in this: While we were still sinners, Christ died for us."

He handed the Bible back. I took it and walked away without another word. I was humiliated. I had found the courage to talk to a homosexual who, I was convinced, was headed straight for hell. Yet he knew more about the Bible than I did. I'd always assumed that anybody who could quote Scripture was a good, solid Christian. For the first time, I realized you don't need God to quote Scripture; you need Him to *live* it.

As I waited now for the deputy to return, I thought about how my memories of Georgia State Penitentiary centered around my relationship with Christ. All of the tough times had helped to boost my faith another notch. Every hardship and obstacle had taught me more about trusting God. He had helped me overcome the trials of prison, and since then had showed me how to use tough faith to help down-and-out teenagers, trust Him for finances when I had no money, and fight the greatest killer I'd ever faced— tougher by far than Bull: Cancer.

It was this tough faith that drove me to tell others about Jesus. Everywhere I looked I saw people locked inside their private prisons: a girl trapped by cerebral palsy; young people driven by peer pressure to have illicit sex because they so desperately wanted love; a man caught in alcohol addiction; a woman forced to endure an unwanted divorce. Peer pressure, poverty, broken families, drugs, illness, and loneliness—these prisons are every bit as real as the cells that confined one thousand men inside

Georgia State Penitentiary. My reason for living was to try to free as many of society's inmates as possible.

My next assignment was Bull Jackson. Humanly, it looked like Mission Impossible. There was no question that this was my most challenging assignment yet. Fortunately, as I prayed, I realized the true challenge had already been met. I had asked to meet Bull by faith, expecting God to do something incredible.

When the deputy returned, he looked serious. "It's cleared," he said. "Let's go see Bull."

Chapter Two

TO SMELL THE ROSES

Security surrounding Bull was tight. We passed through twelve doors on our way to his cell, which was monitored around the clock. The cell was no bigger than a walk-in closet, and the sink and commode took up most of the space. He was standing inside with his back to us as we approached. The deputy hung back to give us some privacy. I took a gulp of water, mouthed a quiet prayer, and then said, "Bull?"

He turned around, revealing a hard, wrinkled face that reminded me of a rabid dog. He was a stout five-foot-ten, with thinning gray hair and a paste-white, though unscarred complexion. His scars, I knew, were beneath his shirt, and he had a significant collection. He'd occasionally taken a knife in the gut, but always came out of fights on top. Even when he looked bad after a brutal attack, the other guy always looked worse.

During my seven years inside this penitentiary, no one frightened me like Bull. And now, his canine-like face resurrected that feeling of dread. "Bull, how you?" I ventured, trying to keep my voice even.

He eyeballed me for a long moment before a look of recognition crossed his face. "Harold Morris," he said slowly. "Harold Morris." His voice sounded like it had been dredged up from his stomach.

"I was just visiting, and found out you were here. I begged the warden to let me come see you."

"You comes back."

I tried to read his inner thoughts. Bull had ice water in his veins, and fifty of the most dangerous men in the world could not scare him. This man couldn't be reasoned with, shouted down, or bullied. His eyes seemed to glow, and looked right through me. I recalled how those eyes always glowed just before he plunged off the deep end.

Standing outside Bull's cell, I hoped he would not remember our old disagreements. I tried to keep the conversation upbeat by talking about his life, and how others perceived him. "I was surprised you were around. I thought you were finished after being shot."

"They knocks me down, but they can't knock me off," he said with pride.

"The warden says he's afraid to let you out into the population."

"They gots me locked up on a bum rap," he growled. "They thinks I'm gunna kill somebody, but I only kills somebody when I gots to. Like the time I tells this guy to get his stuff outa my way, and he wouldn't move it. So I takes care of the problem and does what I gotta. But people, they misunderstands me."

I nodded sympathetically, but felt at loss for what else to say. "Bull, how old you?" I finally asked.

"Sixty-four."

"That so?"

"Yeah, sixty-four."

"Bull, I know you've been here a long time, but how long's it been exactly?"

"Forty-two long ones."

"That's a lifetime."

"I's on my last leg, Harold. The last leg."

I told him I knew the feeling. "Two years ago, I found out I had cancer," I said, showing him the scar on my neck. "They cut out my lymph nodes and have operated twelve times on my throat. I've been blasted with so much radiation that I've lost all my saliva glands, and that's what this water is all about. I have to drink it all the time."

"So you's on your last leg, too?" he asked.

"They say they got it all, but I never know when it might come back."

Bull shook his head. "Everything changes. Ain't the same anymore; not like when you was here."

"How's that?"

"They's a different breed of con today. Ain't like our day. They's younger. They's drug heads. Nobody gives you no respect no more."

I knew Bull was referring to the prestige certain inmates received for their crimes. Murderers and armed robbers got the most respect in the prison hierarchy. Child molesters were on the very bottom rung. In between, men generated varying levels of respect based on their crime, sentence, and ability to defend themselves. But things were changing; many of the young inmates were not willing to abide automatically by the unwritten convict code. I also knew that Bull, despite what he said, got plenty of respect. At age sixty-four, he instilled fear in men forty years his junior.

I realized we didn't have much time, and I couldn't leave without addressing the heavy burden I felt. "Bull, there's something I want to tell you," I said, looking him square in the eye.

"Yeah, what's that?"

For once I wished the bars did not separate us. "Bull, I've got to apologize for being afraid of you. I was always afraid of you in prison, and I was ashamed to share with you about my Lord and Savior, Jesus Christ. I've got to answer for that one day. But let me tell you, Bull—you can spit on me, you can hit me, you can do anything you want to—but I've come today to tell you I love you, and that Jesus died for you. Bull, I'm going to give you the plan of salvation. If it suits your heart would you please respond?"

I briefly told him how, not that many years ago, a fight with another inmate landed me on death row. There, stuck between two killers, I lost all hope. "Unable to live and unable to die," I explained, "I bowed on my knees and prayed, 'God, if You are real, take my life or free me. I can't stand this place anymore.'"

And then I told Bull about my unexpected visit shortly

thereafter from my brother Carl. "Nobody knew where I was, because I was too ashamed to tell them. But he showed up one day out of the blue, followed a few weeks later by Clebe McClary, an old high school friend who had been shot up in Viet Nam. Clebe was missing an arm and missing an eye, and his face had been all patched up after being blown away by grenades. But he still had a heart, and carried a Bible in his right hand—the only hand he still had."

I continued on, describing how those visits launched a series of conversations with loving friends and family members and how, when they shared with me a message of hope in Jesus Christ, a dam of bitterness broke loose. "For the very first time I learned that God loved me," I said, "and also that I was separated from Him because of my sin." And finally I told him how Jesus paid the penalty for our sins by His death on the cross.

"Bull, on February 19, 1974, I knelt in a cell just like this one and cried out to Jesus for forgiveness. He heard my prayer, and He came through the bars and changed my life. A lowly sinner met the mighty Savior! And the same thing can happen to you, Bull. I'm going to say a prayer now, hear? And if you like, Bull, you pray with me. But please, I'm not trying to force anything on you."

I closed my eyes and began to pray. My voice seemed just to bounce off the walls, and I wondered if Bull even had his eyes closed. Or was he staring through me as I prayed? All of a sudden, Bull started repeating the sinner's prayer after me, phrase by phrase. There was a tenderness I'd never heard in his normally sludge-thick voice. When he reached through the bars and grabbed my arms, I couldn't resist opening my eyes. Tears were streaming down his face. All those years he'd been killing people without blinking; now Bull Jackson was crying!

"I's never done nothing like that before," he said when I finished the prayer. "Thank you! Thank you for coming. I'll never forget this day." He squeezed me again through the bars, and I could feel a desperation in his grip. He didn't want to let go.

"Is there anything I can do for you?" I asked.

The ice seemed to melt from his eyes and for the first time, I realized that Bull Jackson knew fear. "I's on my last leg, Harold," he repeated. "Before it's all over, I wants to smell the roses again. I gots me nobody, no family, nobody to sponsor me. Ain't no way they'll parole me without no sponsor or no plan. But I wants to smell the roses, Harold. Just like you. You understands, don't you?"

"I understand, Bull," I said solemnly. He was dying, and needed help. He wanted somebody to care.

"Harold, please don't lets me die here. All I's ask is that they gives me a proper burial. Don't lets 'em bury me in the prison graveyard."

"Bull, I promise I won't." The prison graveyard was the final resting place for inmates whose bodies were not claimed within twenty-four hours. All that marked their years on earth were small crosses with their prison numbers inscribed on them. "I'll talk to the authorities to see what we can arrange. Don't you worry about that."

Bull wiped away a tear with the back of his hand and looked at me with a crooked smile. "Harold Morris, you comes back. You remembers us."

"Yes, Bull. I remember."

"I sees something about you's different. You's changed. Me, nothin' changes. Day after day, until I dies. But I wants to thank you for coming back, Harold. I wants to thank you for not forgetting us."

I told him I would write him and send him a Bible, and assured him I'd return again. Then I turned and walked slowly down the hall, back through the twelve doors that kept Bull Jackson isolated from the world.

My mind was a blur for the next few days. The whole experience seemed incredible. Unreal. Sure, God had dramatically changed my life; He'd changed many lives. But somehow Bull seemed too hardened, too violent, too set in his ways to respond to the Gospel. Sure, I'd prayed before we talked, but never in my wildest imagination could I have anticipated such a response.

Two days after my visit, I received a letter from Bull. "I thought about you all night," he wrote. "The minute I seen you, I knows you was different. You wasn't the same Harold Morris. I'm sorry you got cancer. I's on the last leg of my life, Harold, and I pray that one day I gets to smell the roses before I die. Like you. I wants to also grow me a garden and live in a house." He went on to say that he would pray for me, and thanked me again for visiting him. Then he closed with these words: "Harold, you're the only one that's ever told me about Jesus."

I put Bull's letter down and cried. They were tears of joy and sadness. Joy, because even though I was afraid, I wasn't ashamed of the Gospel of Jesus Christ. He'd given me the courage to open my mouth, and because of that a man who had spent forty-two years in prison would now spend eternity in heaven.

But they were also tears of sadness, because it had taken so long for Bull to hear the Good News. For decades, he'd suffered in a prison of his own making. I knew what that was like; the same thing had happened to me. If it hadn't been for family and friends visiting me and sharing the love of Jesus, who knows how many more years I might have languished in a cell.

What would it take for Bull to break free of his violent anger? He had begun a relationship with Christ, but it was only a start. Without fellowship with other Christians, the support of a church, and discipleship, nothing much would happen. Bull had spent two-thirds of his life in prison. He'd known nothing but violence and hatred. He wouldn't instantly become a loving, kind, considerate human being.

Nevertheless, Bull could change—by God's grace and by exercising tough faith. Tough faith was the key that opened any prison—the physical penitentiary as well as the private cells that bound much of society. For Bull, the bars and razor wire were visible reminders of his incarceration. But people all around me were just as trapped by their past or present hurts. And without tough faith, their futures were equally bleak.

Just what is tough faith? The Bible says it "is being sure of what we hope for and certain of what we do not see" (Hebrews 11:1). Tough faith is sticking with God in difficult situations. It pulls us through disease, heartache, and tragedy. It gives us a reason for living and helps us face depression, loneliness, broken relationships, and all the little hurts we endure daily. It allows us to be parents to our children, lovers to our spouse, and friends to those who are unlovely. It could transform Bull Jackson—as it did Harold Morris—even though he might never leave the confines of Georgia State Penitentiary. In short, tough faith enables us to break through any barrier life throws at us, and see the victory.

For me, tough faith grew in tough circumstances: in prison, in a boys' home, in times of financial need, in excruciating physical pain, even when faced with death. It didn't just happen. It was nurtured during my early years as a Christian, amidst persecution and temptation. That's when tough faith first helped me bust through some barriers that had nearly ruined my life.

In prison, Christians were viewed as weak. Inmates delighted in trying to make us fall. They took advantage of us, stole our few possessions, tried to provoke us to fight, and treated us as less than human. Everywhere we turned, there were numerous temptations, and I surrendered to many.

For example, I was introduced to drugs in prison. I particularly enjoyed smoking marijuana. It was a nice escape from my drab existence. For a few minutes, I could enjoy the high. I had no problems. I forgot the guards and had no enemies. It was easy to rationalize, "How could a little marijuana hurt anybody?" Inevitably, at the moment I was weakest someone would come by the cell and say, "Hey man, got some good stuff to smoke if you're up to it."

Saying no to the drugs didn't come easy after I met Christ. Every time I yielded, I felt intense guilt. I'd lie on my bunk for hours at night, hearing my conscience say, "That was wrong." Thus would begin a tug-of-war between Jesus and Satan, with me as the rope.

One voice would argue, "Hey, it's no big deal. You ain't ever going to get out of prison, so go ahead. It's just a little joint. What harm can that do?"

Then guilt would settle on me: "You're a disgrace to your family. You should be ashamed even to call yourself a Christian."

How I longed for some strong Christian friend who would take time to talk with me, pray with me, and help me through these struggles. But there was no such person in the penitentiary.

The tug-of-war raged day after day, leaving me emotionally stretched and exhausted. Many times I tried to defeat Satan on my own. I always lost. Gradually, I began to realize it was only through Christ that I had the strength and power to resist temptation. I read one day in 1 John 4:4, "You, dear children, are from God and have overcome them, because the one who is in you is greater than the one who is in the world." It was time to start heeding the still, small voice of God instead of the nagging, tempting voice of Satan.

I was led to prison in the first place precisely because I had made a habit of listening to the wrong voice. As a Christian, I had to stop seeing how much I could sin without getting caught. Jesus once said that anyone who wanted to follow Him had to carry a cross. The cross was an instrument of death. Jesus was nailed to one. The same thing had to happen to my vanity, ego, pride, and all of the other things that were contrary to God's will in my life.

One day my cellmate offered me a hit, and I shook my head. "No, I'm through," I said.

He just laughed. "You'll smoke again. Just wait, you'll come back."

"No, I'm through for good."

I didn't *feel* like saying no. But saying no anyway was a small victory that strengthened me for the next temptation. Gradually, as I said no enough times, the opportunity for drugs dried up because people simply stopped offering them to me. I even heard some say, "Super Honky's gone straight. He quit dope, so don't even bother asking." It was ironic that junky inmates would help me stay off drugs. And so I learned an important lesson about faith: Say no long enough, and the people tempting you will lose interest and go try to ruin somebody else's life.

There were so many lessons to learn, and some of them were very difficult because they involved wrong reactions developed over years of practice. For instance, my temper inevitably led to fights whenever I was provoked. One evening, I was enjoying a rare moment of quiet in my cell. At the time, I had two cell-mates—Frito, the only Puerto Rican in the prison, who was serving a twenty-year sentence for robberies he'd pulled to support a drug habit; and Phantom, who had supposedly committed 150 rapes. Both were away for the moment, and I was hoping they'd stay away until lock-up at eight o'clock. It provided some rare free time for me to study the Bible in peace.

Suddenly both of them stumbled into the cell, so loaded on drugs they looked like they could fly. When Frito saw my open Bible, he started hassling me in broken English. "Hey, Jesus freak. Hey, man, Jesus freak." He repeated those words, and Phantom quickly joined in.

My old sin nature started to boil. My aggressiveness rose to the surface. In the middle of their little jive routine, I attacked. Forgetting what I held in my hand, I clubbed both of them with my Bible. Frito stumbled backward and crashed against the wall. Phantom covered his head and cowered in a corner.

As I raised my arm to strike more blows, I suddenly realized what I was doing. I stopped, stared at my Bible, and then stepped back in shock. "Please forgive me," I said immediately. "You've got to forgive me."

"Hey man, you call yourself a *Christian*?" Frito sneered. "You're no different than me."

I sat on my bunk as tears filled my eyes. I knew my actions were not the proper Christian response to Frito's taunting, but I protested, "I *am* different. You'll see." Both of them laughed.

"Please, you've got to forgive me," I repeated. "I *am* a Christian. You don't know my heart. I'll do anything to make this right. I didn't mean it."

Now they were really laughing. "You gotta forgive me," bellowed Frito. "I didn't mean it," mocked Phantom. They were practically rolling on the ground.

I knew it was futile to say any more, so I faced the wall to hide my shame. "God, help me!" I prayed. "I didn't choose my cellmates. I'm locked in here with a drug addict and a rapist. They aren't believers. And now I've beaten them over the head with my Bible."

Though I felt like the worst Christian in the world, I began to see how God was subtly changing my life. I recognized it was only because of His grace that I didn't hit my cellmates with something else. There had been a time when I belted men with a mop bucket handle or beat them senseless with my fists. So God was working on me. Still, I never wanted to hit anyone again, much less with a Bible.

I was proud to be a Christian, and each stand I took strengthened my faith. One day I arrived at my prison job, and the man I was replacing laughed at me as he shouted to one of the guards, "Lieutenant, you'd better watch what you say around ol' Harold cuz he's a Christian."

I walked right up to him and stuck my face in his. "What did you say?" I challenged.

"I said you'd better watch yourself around ol' Harold. He's a Christian."

This was a typical prison confrontation prior to a fight. I could tell he was anticipating it. But I looked him straight in the eye, and said, "You just paid me the highest compliment I've ever received. And I want you to know I'm changing my life. I'm not going to be the same person."

Of course, there could be no fight after those words. The con and the lieutenant thought this was hilarious. The guard was laughing so hard he was shaking. "Ol' Super Honky, he's done everything else, so now he's going to try religion."

I turned on the guard and launched a different kind of attack. "I don't know why you laughing. You're in prison as much as I am."

"How's that?"

"You've been here fourteen years. That's seven more years than I've done. You live right here on the reservation. You're on call twenty-four hours a day. You work six days a week. You've told me how miserable your family life is. You complain every day. The only thing you exist for is fishing.

"Now look at me. You don't hear me complaining anymore. I've learned how to be happy right where I am. I know God will let me out when He's ready to, and no one will be able to stop

Him. Until then, I'm content to serve Him here. So who's in prison? You or me?"

The guard gave me a sheepish look and shook his head. "I have to admit you make sense. I'm in debt real bad and won't be able to send my kids to college. You are more free than me." He turned and walked away, and I felt sadness knowing that this man had put himself in prison. He couldn't even tell his wife and kids he loved them, while I was free to express my love to all those around me. That was how much God had changed my life—my tough faith that was growing.

One crucial factor in the maturing process was time spent alone, reading my Bible and praying. I didn't want my Christianity to be another passing phase. I wanted it to last. But quiet times were hard to find in prison. There were always inmates in my cell. There was constant noise and interruptions. The TV was always blasting. There was so much yelling and cussing that you could hardly concentrate. Someone down the line would be banging on his cell door, shouting, "Hey, give me a cigarette here." Someone else would yell at him to shut up. It seemed like a day couldn't pass without several fights and at least one brawl. And in the summer the cells were so hot and smelled so bad it made your eyes cross.

Somehow I had to get away from the crowd. I noticed that even Jesus slipped away from the demands of the multitudes and His disciples, and got alone in the desert or on a mountainside to be with His Father. I concluded that in or out of prison, I would need a sanctuary, a place to be alone. In prison there were two sanctuaries where I found a little peace. One was the shower, and there I would pray and have a quiet time. I called it "power in the shower." As I stood under the water, I came clean in more ways than one. In prayer, I would admit my sins as they came to mind and allow God to wash them away as He promised He would.

The other refuge was the athletic shed, a small room just off the chapel where all the athletic equipment was stored. Since I was in charge of the prison's athletic programs and issued all the equipment to the inmates, I would go there often. The shed was about twenty by thirty feet, and I had shelves built along the walls to hold all of the boxing gear, baseball gloves, softball equipment, volleyballs, nets, and shuffleboard sets. This was the one place in the prison that didn't stink. The smells of the leather gloves and balls were like perfume to me. Entering the shed was like driving into the mountain-fresh air and leaving the smog of a dirty city behind. There were times I wished I could bottle the aroma and take it back to my cell.

Using a folding chair and a big cardboard box for a desk, I studied the Bible. Here the Scriptures began to make sense as I got to know the Lord and what He wanted me to do. I'd analyze a passage and, with the help of a concordance, flip to other verses to better understand what it meant. Then I would think about how to use what I learned in my life that day.

Applying those lessons were never easy. For example, I became convinced that God wanted me to seek forgiveness when I wronged someone. That meant humbling myself in a place where admitting fault was unheard of. But I never had any peace until I made my wrong right. During the five years I'd been in prison before I became a Christian, I'd never told anyone I was sorry. In my mind, the other guy was always wrong. If someone crossed me, my first thought was to kill him. I never actually did, but I put a few in the hospital. Then I'd stew for days afterward, thinking, "You idiot, Morris, you should have killed him. The world would be better off without him."

Then I read in the Bible that "if anyone is in Christ, he is a new creation; the old has gone, the new has come!" (2 Cor. 5:17). The Holy Spirit had come into my life and was booting out the old way of thinking and behaving. Sin was being chased out the door. Unfortunately, some of those sins ran around a little while before they headed for the exit!

Several times I lost my temper on the basketball court. We played by modified jungle rules whereby one had to accept a busted nose, dislocated shoulder, or cracked ribs as part of the game. It enabled inmates to let off steam without killing a guy. But sometimes I'd take a wayward elbow personally, and start yelling. As soon as I calmed down, I'd go up to the other guy—

even if his gross foul had been deliberate, and say, "Will you forgive me for blowing my cool?" The player would look at me like I was on drugs. So I'd repeat myself, "Will you forgive me?" Whether or not he'd respond, I'd finally say, "I love you and look forward to playing with you tomorrow." The other players never got used to it; they were convinced I was one step away from the funny farm.

One morning I got mad at my cellmate, Phantom. He had deceived me. Both of us had done some speaking to schools outside of the prison. An invitation came one day and Phantom told me the warden had told him I couldn't go. Later I learned the warden wasn't even in his office that day. I challenged Phantom on it. "You're a liar," I said.

"No, you're the liar," he retorted, even though he knew I was right. "I'm through with you."

"Let me tell you what I think of you," I said, proceeding to use a few choice words so he'd clearly understand my message. Most of those words would have been better left unsaid.

Phantom didn't speak to me the rest of the day. He wasn't a Christian, and I had earlier tried to win him to the Lord. My anger wasn't drawing him any closer. That night the tension in our cell weighed on me like the humid Georgia air. I tried to sleep but couldn't. My conscience was working double-time. I asked God to forgive me and to give me the strength to overcome the temptations. But that wasn't enough. Then I remembered the instructions of Scripture: if you have a problem with someone, go to him and make it right.

About three o'clock in the morning, I said to Phantom, "Hey buddy, I'm sorry. It was wrong for me to talk to you like I did today. You've got to forgive me. I love you."

Phantom was awake, and I noticed his voice tremble as he said, "Thank you, Harold. I needed that. I couldn't sleep, either. I love you like a brother. You mean more to me than anybody in my life."

We both stood up and hugged each other. I knew then I was on the right track. Though we were in a prison cell with five life sentences between us, we were learning how to love each other.

Resisting drugs, asking my cellmates to forgive me, standing proudly for my faith against the taunts of inmates and guards, faithfully praying, reading my Bible, and humbly confessing my sins to God and those I had offended were the daily manifestations of faith that needed to operate whether I was in prison or out. My faith was weak, but it was growing tougher. It eventually broke through my macho shield. No longer was I afraid to reach out and say, "Hey, man, I'm sorry," and pray with a guy. I began to care about people. And others noticed, even the guards. I was different. I was a new man.

Chapter Three

PREPARATION BEFORE PERFORMANCE

Watching television with a ragtag bunch of convicts seemed like a strange way to learn some important lessons about faith. Even more surprising was finding that groups of men occasionally watched religious programming. For some, it was a sentimental reminder of their youth—of a mother or grandmother who had listened to radio preachers or attended revivals. Others found certain off-beat preachers a source of entertainment. Between all the hoots, expletives, obscene commentary, and belches, I discovered what faith most certainly was not.

The Christian life many of the television preachers talked about was exactly the opposite of my experience in prison. I'd found that faith, to survive, must be tough. Their faith seemed easy. Theirs was the gospel of prosperity and good times. Mine was the gospel of hard knocks and heartache. I was thoroughly confused. Even their Jesus seemed different from mine.

Once I watched a television evangelist speak before a huge crowd about the dangers of tobacco and drugs, when he suddenly announced, "There's somebody up in the balcony who's got a pack of Kools. Bring those Kools down. Right now, get out of your seat and throw them away!" A few moments later somebody actually came forward and tossed the cigarettes on the stage. Then the preacher said, "And there's some of you who've got drugs. You come down, too." Even as he talked, people began walking to the front and throwing their drugs on stage.

Among the group watching the program that day was one of the big drug runners in prison. When he saw the pile of dope on the stage, he announced, "When I get out, I'm heading straight to that guy's church for a score!"

I watched other television preachers raise huge sums of money by talking about God's love for prisoners. I knew about God's love, but these manicured mannequins with their makeup and blow-dried hairdos tried to sound as if they, too, cared. If they cared so much, how come they didn't visit the prisons themselves? Where were they?

Another television preacher was big on healings. "If you're in pain, just get out of your chair and come lay your hands on your television, and we'll pray for your release," he hollered. Some of the other inmates got a hoot out of that, and they paraded up to the TV, laughing and carrying on about how God would spring them from prison. Then at the end of the service we heard a deep baritone voice announce, "This program has been pre-recorded." My friends thought that was an absolute scream. I thought it was sad, because the Christianity they saw on television reflected on my faith. And I didn't see much connection between the two.

The guys on television with the most jewelry always seemed to be the ones who talked most about money. "Give to our ministry, and God will bless you," they'd say. "Give now, and it shall be given to you." They said the money you sent would "plant a seed." That bothered me, because I noticed that the seed was always planted in *their* garden. Why couldn't somebody visit Georgia State Penitentiary and plant some seeds there? Instead, I suspected the money was spent to fund another limo for the preacher.

There was one guy on television who we watched nearly every Sunday. One day it was announced that he was coming to the prison, along with two singers from his program. I couldn't believe it. A televangelist *did* care. They showed up at our chapel a few weeks later, but only fourteen inmates were in the audience. We were scheduled to have an hour service from ten to eleven o'clock, but at a quarter past ten, the preacher was still waiting for more to come.

The silence got a little awkward, so one of the inmates finally said he thought nobody else was coming, and that we probably ought to get the show on the road.

The preacher looked at him, cleared his throat, and checked his watch. He motioned us all up into the first two rows, and checked his watch again. "I'm real sorry about this, but we're going to need to speed things along this morning," he said. "I've got another engagement, and we're sort of in a hurry. So I hope you don't mind if I talk for just a few minutes and we skip the singing."

He thought he had us fooled, but the state didn't take away our brains when we entered prison. The problem was not time, but numbers. He wanted a full house. Because there was barely a dozen of us, he was gone in less than thirty minutes. I left that "service" in a state of disillusionment, and for a long time I distrusted all televangelists.

So much of what these preachers talked about seemed contrary to my own experience, and that fact confused me as a young Christian. As I studied more of the Bible, I read the Apostle Paul's words on this very issue. In 1 Timothy 1:1-11, he wrote about those who "teach false doctrines" and "promote controversies rather than God's work." I began to see that people could use Christianity for their own selfish prosperity, and that money could be diverted to serve their own causes rather than to proclaim the Gospel. Fortunately, not all ministers were this way.

Through this I realized that I had a responsibility to be faithful to what God wanted me to do. I read Paul's claim in 1 Timothy 1:12-17, that "Christ Jesus our Lord . . . considered me faithful, appointing me to his service." In my mind, there was no higher calling than to serve God and teach others that "Christ Jesus came into the world to save sinners." I disregarded the mumbo jumbo about laying hands on the television and planting seeds. The important thing was that Jesus saves. And if He could save and use Saul of Tarsus, the chief of sinners, then He could save and use Harold Morris, the chief of sinners today.

Certainly there were plenty of candidates for miraculous conversions in prison. But I hardly knew what I believed, much less how to witness. Reading the Bible and praying helped a great deal, but that was not enough. I had read in the Bible that it was important for Christians to gather together regularly. In other words, I needed to go to church. At Georgia State Penitentiary, there was no church in the building which I was in. Prisoners worked seven days a week, and authorities figured church would only be an excuse for men to skip work. A retired minister did come and lead a service on Thursday evenings, but hardly anyone attended. The first time I went, only eight other inmates were there, and I was the only white. The preacher mostly shouted his sermons, which were full of references to sin and Judgment Day. He gave us very little information about how to grow as Christians, but bombarded us about how we'd roast as sinners. I knew I needed more solid teaching; I also needed the strength of other committed believers. Unfortunately, there was precious little I could do about either of those issues.

At that point, I realized I had a choice to make. I could complain about my situation in prison, or I could accept it and learn to be a witness for God right where I was. I knew that if I didn't serve Him behind bars, I wouldn't serve Him when I was released. And if I wanted more Christian friends, certainly one way to find them was to win them to Christ.

That was when I tried my ill-conceived witness to Peaches, which showed me how little I really understood about my faith. I'd had the courage to speak up, which was a good first step. But when I opened my mouth, I stuck my foot in it. After enduring Peaches' mocking laugh, I told myself, *This will never happen again*. I vowed that I would spend as much time as possible studying the Bible, getting to know it backward and forward. I had a lot to learn. But next time I would be ready. "Preparation before performance," became my motto.

The turning point was a discipleship program sponsored by Campus Crusade for Christ, called the Lay Institute for Evangelism. It was led by a group of businessmen and was the first long-term teaching program officials had ever allowed in the prison. The lay leaders came to the prison every Tuesday night for three months, and concluded with a final session that lasted fifty-four hours over a three-day weekend.

The leader was a hospital administrator who lived nearby in the town of Reidsville. I was impressed with how much he cared for our small ragtag group. He was also an exceptional teacher with a tremendous knowledge of Scripture. Of course, at that time, I would have been impressed with anybody who knew five verses and could differentiate all the Johns in the Bible.

This was the first real discipleship I received. I had grown a lot on my own during the previous three years, and I was ready for more. His teaching was over the heads of many of the inmates. Some were too proud to admit they couldn't read or write, and left early. But a majority stayed through the course. The highlight for me was a film series by Dr. Bill Bright, Campus Crusade for Christ president and founder, who taught fundamental Bible truths such as "How to be sure you are a Christian" and "How to live each day in the power of the Holy Spirit."

That final weekend our leader announced, "To get your completion certificate, you must witness to five people by next Thursday." He gave us a questionnaire to use to help spark conversation, and copies of "The Four Spiritual Laws" booklet to aid with presentation of the Gospel. I wanted the certificate, because I knew it would look good when I was considered for parole. I figured I would just talk with some sissy prisoners, and be done with the formality.

But lying in my cell that night, I felt convicted. I said to myself, *No, I'm going to pick out the most dangerous men at this institution, men that nobody has ever witnessed to, and tell them about Jesus.* I decided I'd approach the badest of the bad, and singled out five men: Railroad, Big Money, Cow Daddy, Burrhead, and Big Lip. I was frightened by this decision, but I remembered our teaching. I would approach them in the power of the Holy Spirit, and leave the results to God.

The first guy I approached was Railroad, a 250-pound man with a long railroad-track scar running from his left ear to the corner of his mouth. He'd been in prison nineteen years on his latest sentence, and could put a chill down your spine just by stepping into the same room. He was a killer, pure and simple. One night he told a nineteen-year-old kid to quit playing the guitar so he could go to sleep. But the kid wouldn't stop. So Railroad got up, ripped one of the guitar strings off the instrument, and hung him on the bars. Several other inmates watched the kid die, but no one ever squealed because they all knew the same thing would happen to them.

I finally got my courage up and invited Railroad to my cell for a Pepsi. "Got something I'd like to talk to you about," I said, trying to sound nonchalant.

"Yeah, okay," he said.

At the appointed hour, Railroad came up to my cell and sat on the opposite bunk. I gave him a Pepsi, then got out the questionnaire. It had twenty questions. The first question was: "Are you a Christian?" I said a silent prayer as I wished this question could have been last. But there was no turning back now.

I swallowed hard and began, "Railroad, I'm going to this Bible study group, and I've been given a form to fill out that I need your help with." He nodded, belched, and took another swig of Pepsi. "I need to ask you some questions, and hey, all I need are some answers. No sweat, huh?"

He gave me the eye, and said, "Shoot." I was so scared that if I'd had a gun, I just might have taken him up on it.

"First question, Railroad." I paused to take a deep breath. "Are you a Christian?"

"*What* you say?" he growled.

"No problem, I'll just put 'no' right here," I said faintly.

"You know I ain't no Christian."

"That's right, I know that. But it's a question I have to ask, and now I'll just write 'no' in the box."

The rest of the questions weren't any easier. When I finished I said, "Railroad, I admire you very much, and I wonder if you'd do me a favor?"

He just grunted, so I continued quickly. "One thing I like about you is that you're a man of your word. If you say you're going to kill somebody, you kill 'em. You do what you say."

"Do my best," he said.

"I wonder if you'd take this little booklet." I pulled "The Four Spiritual Laws" booklet from my back pocket. "Would you take this, go back to your cell, and promise me that within the next twenty-four hours you'll read it? And would you give me your word that you'll come back to my cell with some sort of response? You can spit on me, you can hit me, but would you respond in some way?"

"Yeah," he grumbled, "I'll do that." He grabbed the booklet and left.

After Railroad, I approached the other four inmates in quick succession. First was Big Money, a tall, handsome, sandy blond in his late twenties. When asked how he got his nickname, he'd respond, "When you're sick, you go to a doctor; when you need legal advice, you go to an attorney; when you need money, you go to the bank." Big Money was a bank robber. He derived status from the fact that he robbed banks and dealt with "professionals," and he looked down on those who knocked off service stations and convenience stores.

Next on my list was Cow Daddy, who worked on the prison dairy detail and fell in love with cow #484. The cows were identified numerically just like the inmates, and had their numbers branded on their flanks and stamped on ear tags. Cow Daddy was jet black, in his early fifties, and covered with scars from numerous knifings. He'd have killed anybody who touched his cow, and most inmates feared him enough to stay away from the barn altogether.

Burrhead was the fourth inmate on my list. A convicted rapist, he was a small, uneducated white guy, with stiff, closely-cropped hair. He was country all the way, and had a "y'all" twang in his voice that was as thick as grits. Upon entering Georgia State Penitentiary, he switched sexual orientation, and took a liking to young boys.

Finally, I spoke with Big Lip, a tall, well-built black man who had a bottom lip that practically hung down to his chin. He drove tractors and trucks around the institution, and inmates would say that he once stuck his head out of a dump truck window and was nearly beaten to death by his lip. About forty, Big Lip had a murder rap against him, and had been there many years. He was an awful-looking sight, not only because of his lips but because he often wrapped his head with a woman's nylon and wore a short-billed prison cap sideways over that.

All five of those desperados were dangerous, and most had served more than ten years. I called them the "Unholy Five," because they wouldn't have been caught dead in church. It was an indescribable relief when the last one left my cell. I jumped up, and gave a shout. I'd survived in one piece. I was still alive.

Then the most amazing thing happened. During the next week, all five of those men responded. Each of them returned to my cell just as I'd asked. Big Money threw the booklet on the bed and said, "This junk ain't for me." Cow Daddy was more polite: "I appreciate what you said, but I'm not much for religion." I thanked them profusely for coming back.

When the other three returned to my cell, I was still nervous. Most people wouldn't have thought of stopping them to talk about the Lord. When I asked Railroad for his response, he said matter-of-factly, "Harold, if it's good enough for you, it's good enough for me." Then miracle of miracles, he and the others bowed their heads and prayed to receive Christ! Because of that, to this day Romans 1:16 is one of my favorite verses: "I am not ashamed of the Gospel, because it is the power of God for the salvation of everyone who believes."

What was even more amazing to me was that God started using me *outside* of prison while I was still incarcerated. One day the warden called me to his office and told me that a local high school had asked him if an inmate could speak to the students about alcohol, drugs, and prison life. Of 3,200 inmates, he selected me. That was the first of many such talks, and other inmates also started speaking. In a one-year period, I spoke to ten thousand students and adults in high schools, colleges, churches, and service clubs.

Because of the hopelessness of my prison cell, I took my outside speaking very seriously. I knew that each time I spoke might be my last chance. So I spent hours perfecting my message, realizing I might not have another shot at helping those people.

As a result of these appearances, I began receiving hundreds of letters. Many were from kids who needed help. And to think that for my first five years in prison, I never got a single letter!

The first time I was asked to speak in a church, I was very nervous. Apparently, many of the kids who had heard me previously at school told their friends about me. The church was packed. I spoke for an hour, presenting my testimony about how God had touched my life while I was in prison. At the close of the service, the pastor gave an altar call, and many came forward to receive Christ.

God could and was using me while I was still behind bars, and I realized He would continue to use me as long as I was faithful to Him. That helped when I experienced setbacks in my attempts to be released. One school teacher in Douglas, a community where I did a lot of speaking, was obsessed with obtaining my freedom. He was joined by a number of friends who pursued every appropriate legal channel. But their efforts only led them to dead ends. So I had a lot of time to practice serving God faithfully right where I was.

I arranged for a crusade in the prison featuring my spiritual father Lt. Clebe McClary, who had a hook for one arm and a permanent patch over his left eye. One hundred and twenty men packed our little chapel like sardines. And that day sixty-six trusted Christ. I followed up with all of them, giving each a Bible.

The following afternoon, one of the blacks who had prayed to receive Christ during the service approached me in the athletic shed. "You know, yesterday I didn't want to go to that church service," he began. "I didn't believe in that junk. But I watched that man's beautiful white wife walk by, and I got the sudden urge to go."

After that crack, he got serious. "During the service, I sat there and looked around at all these murderers and robbers and rapists, wondering what the heck I was doing there. Then afterward, that speaker walked up to me and put his white arm around me. He looked at me with his one good eye and told me he loved me. I couldn't believe it! Ain't nobody—especially a white—ever told me they love me. That man's different. He's real. And he ain't a bad preacher for a white boy!"

We both laughed at that, and then I asked him about his response to Clebe's challenge to follow Christ. "When he talked about being a Christian, I wanted to cry cuz I knew I wasn't," he answered. "Then I looked on my left, and the dude next to me was crying. The dude to my right was also crying. So I got on my knees, gave my heart to Christ like he was talking about, and then I started crying. And you know what, Super Honky?"

"What's that?"

"Super Honk, I want to tell you something. I love you, man! I've hated whites all my life, but I love you. I'll say it again, man. I love you. And I want you to tell that speaker I love him."

He gave a loud cackle and stuck out his hand. I slapped it and then stuck out my palm for him to slap. And then with a grin big enough to crack a face, he walked away to continue enjoying his first day as a new Christian.

Even more encouraging was what happened to my cellmates Frito and Phantom, the two men I'd beaten over the head with my Bible. The Puerto Rican had come to the crusade because, like Clebe, he'd been in the Marines. After the service, I asked Clebe to talk with him for a minute. Clebe put his hook on Frito's shoulder, and I could see my cellmate begin to soften.

After the service, I followed Frito back to the cell and found him in a very sober mood. "It's happened," he said to me. "I don't know what's happened to me, but it's happened." I knew exactly what had happened. He'd had his first encounter with the living Christ.

Phantom, who had also been touched, then told me, "You know, my dad was a preacher for thirty-nine years." Tears welled up in his eyes, but he wouldn't let them flow. I knew his father had died while he was in prison. "I killed my daddy," he said. "It broke his heart when I went to prison."

A few months later, Phantom was transferred to a work-release center. Just before he left, he told me, "I want you to know that

I've trusted Christ." He never told me how, but I knew he was serious. Maybe something sunk in when I clobbered him with my Bible!

In addition to my bold witness inside the penitentiary, there was another evidence of my faith, perhaps the most obvious change to me personally. It was the peace I could enjoy even in the midst of that hell. I felt it most during yard call. At one o'clock every afternoon, the bell would ring and all of us working inside the prison would file into the yard. When the sun was shining, I would head over to a small grove of bushy old pecan trees. Underneath was some grass where I could lie and look beyond the razor wire and chain link fence to the woods and fields surrounding the prison complex.

Most of the inmates headed for the perimeter of the yard to pace along the beaten path against the fence. They seemed like animals in a zoo, walking in a circle as close to freedom as many of them would ever get. I had done the same when I'd first arrived, but that changed after I invited Christ into my life. I went from being a bitter, desperate person who lived off hatred, rebelled against authority, barked at God like a dog, and thought constantly of escape to one who finally recognized the beauty that had always been around him.

As I lay on the grass, I could see all the guard towers, the officers in them armed with high-powered rifles. But beyond the towers and the razor wire were trees and wildflowers. I'd think of the deer grazing in those woods and how they were free. In my imagination, I'd see them jumping gracefully over a fallen log, or sipping from a small stream. And as I did, a wave of peace would wash over me.

Often I'd look up at the guards standing high above us and think, "I wouldn't trade places with them for anything in the world." They were prisoners just like the rest of us. Some of them even lived on the prison compound and were on twenty-four hour call. But I was free! For me, the prison walls, the bars, and razor wire were invisible. I had a peace and joy I'd never before experienced. Though all my rights had been stripped from me, and I was officially a ward of the state, yet I was able to see and experience God's creation for the first time. Amidst all the hatred, bitterness, and loneliness of prison life, surrounded by heartache, depravity, and depression, I was overwhelmed by a sense of God's presence.

Under those pecan trees I learned one of the most important lessons about faith. I discovered that neither freedom nor happiness depends on outward circumstances. I was as free at those times as I would ever be if I someday was allowed to walk outside the walls of this prison. Nothing in life—good looks, a fancy home, or big paychecks—*nothing* could satisfy me any more than the peace of Christ. Still, I longed for the day when I would be free physically, to be able to walk barefoot down the beach, to wander through a forest, to walk through the front door of my mother's home and give her a big hug.

Often I looked up in the sky at the billowy clouds. In the distance I might see thunderheads building up in the afternoon heat. But the clouds above were soft, reminding me of sheep grazing peacefully in a field. As I gazed into these cloud formations, I pictured the faces of people whom I knew and loved. The one face I imagined most often was that of my dear mother. I'd think how good she was, and how I'd never heard her say a bad word about anybody. I tried to picture what she was doing, and wondered whether she'd die while I was in prison. I knew that was likely, since I'd received a double-life sentence, but I didn't want her heartache about me to kill her.

A mother was the only person near and dear to most inmates. Mothers offered a special kind of love, because they loved you no matter what. Even the most dangerous inmates often had a MOM tattoo on their arms. That was because mothers never gave up. Other family members would disown you because you'd disgraced them. Fathers would write you off in a minute, never stopping to think that they might have failed their sons by never being home, working all hours, or carousing at night. But a mother would cry herself to sleep, blaming herself for her son's crimes. She would never stop loving. I was convinced that nobody was fully an animal while he still had a mother living.

Though my mother had always supported me without any

strings attached, I was ashamed to contact her when I was arrested, even though the charges were false. I maintained my silence for five years, not wanting her to know I had wound up in prison. She'd always told me I'd become a somebody. In prison I felt like a nobody until I met Christ.

Then my brother finally learned where I was and visited me. He told me Mom was worried and asked me to call her. I was allowed to make a five-minute collect call. As soon as my mother came on the line, I said to her, "Mother, I love you. I'm sorry I let you down." And she answered, "Son, you be a good boy. I love you and pray for you every day."

Often as I stared at the clouds I'd ask God to let me live to see my mother again, and prayed that He not let her die while I was behind bars. I wanted to love her back, to try and give her some peaceful years before she died. Words and letters weren't enough. I wanted her to have the joy of knowing me as a Christian son and seeing me witnessing for Christ. I wanted to show her that she was right, that I had become *somebody*.

Inside my head, a little voice would say, "That will never happen. You will never see your mother. You're going to die here." I was prepared to die in prison, yet I hoped and prayed for a different outcome. I wanted to be free again for her.

Inevitably that time of peace in the yard would end. The bell would ring and we would return to the drab, noisy metal and concrete cells that were our homes. There the reality of my environment would crowd in and try to convince me that those peaceful moments with God were just a figment of my imagination. But they were real, and I knew it.

At the time I didn't realize God had a plan and purpose for me that went far beyond my highest hope or dreams. But preparation had to come before performance. There were many lessons to learn, and every hardship and obstacle was there for a reason—to further strengthen my faith. Every time I tried to solve a problem myself, I failed. But God never failed me. When I exercised tough faith, He worked miraculously in my life and the lives of men around me. Of course, there were many more lessons to learn about faith. Soon God would enable me to learn and apply them in a wider arena.

Chapter Four

HANDLE WITH LOVE

After years of persistent efforts by friends and family, my release from prison finally came on March 14, 1978. During the last few hours of my incarceration, I thanked the Lord for this miracle and for the precious people who cared so much about me. And most of all, I was careful to give God the credit for my parole. As I was being processed and awaiting my triumphant walk through the front gate, Warden R. B. Thompson came up to me. Over the years, we'd had a lot of contact and I greatly respected him. He'd assigned me to the athletic department, let me teach Spanish to inmates, and once took me with him in his pickup to mark off the rifle range for the guards. He even brought his eight-year-old son into the prison and allowed him to visit my cell.

I was honored that the warden trusted me. But I never took that trust for granted. He was a stern disciplinarian whose bottom line was, "I'll break you if you mess with me." Inmates who talked back to him would land in solitary confinement so fast their heads would spin. Sometimes I could talk him out of a rash decision. I'd say, "Come on now, Mr. Thompson. The man's got problems and didn't mean to spout off. I'll go talk to him and get him to cool down. Please give him another chance."

Approaching me as I was about to leave, the warden said, "Harold, you have the second best record of anyone here, but I'd have bet anything that you'd have served a minimum of twenty years before you were paroled. Who did you pay off?"

I flashed a big smile, motioned for him to come close, and then whispered, "Jesus Christ!"

The warden shook his head and walked away. There was no doubt in my mind that Jesus Christ had freed me. It was an answer to my prayers and the dogged persistence of many friends.

Before I left the prison I said good-bye to my fellow inmates, many of whom were jealous of my release. I could tell by their expressions that they were wondering, "Why you? What makes you so special that you were paroled and not me?"

Two things: I'd never committed the crimes I'd originally been charged with, and I was a child of the King!

Upon release from prison, you must be paroled to a "home" of some sorts. You can't just wander the streets, or move to the opposite coast to begin a new life. In my case, I was paroled to a boys' home in Orangeburg, South Carolina. While still in prison, I'd sent some leather wallets to the home and asked that they be sold to buy clothes for the kids. The director, who knew my friends Clebe McClary and Bobby Richardson, former New York Yankee baseball star, visited the prison and got to know me. Together they formulated a plan for me to work at the boys' home upon my release.

Before leaving Georgia State Penitentiary, I'd made a statement that all I wanted in life was a chance to share love. Now I had my chance. I could become a loving, supportive father to dozens of boys who had no father. In addition, I would be paid a whopping six thousand dollars a year!

The boys' home was situated in a beautiful pastoral setting, with brick buildings, a cafeteria, gymnasium, pecan trees, and a lake. It had about fifty acres of rich, flat land, which was leased to soybean, corn and peanut farmers to help support the institution. There were four apartments on the property, which were shared by the teachers and me. Mine was a small, brick-exterior, two-bedroom unit furnished with hand-me-downs from the Salvation Army and various churches. It had a couch with fraying brown cushions, a black vinyl chair with a gaping hole in the seat, one old lamp, and a bed with an old saggy mattress that touched the floor when I laid down. But I had no complaints; to me, it felt like a palace. I was happy to finally have a place of my own to call home for the first time in ten years.

When I arrived I was greeted by bright yellow ribbons the boys had tied around the pecan trees, and a big sign that said, "Welcome Home Mr. Morris." It was one of the most touching moments of my life. I knew then I was where God wanted me. Here I'd be loved, and here I'd have a chance to share love with thirty-six kids, ages eight through eighteen. But there were adjustments to be made and barriers to overcome for us all.

One major adjustment was learning to live within the rules of parole. I wasn't a citizen of the United States. I couldn't be out past midnight, and couldn't go anywhere before six in the morning. To leave the city limits, I needed advance permission, and I had to report in person to my parole officer once a month. It was like being a high school student all over again, with my mother second-guessing my every move.

There also wasn't the "security" of prison where most all important decisions are made for you: what to eat, when to sleep, what job to work. It was a major adjustment making those decisions for myself. The day I was released from prison, my brother took me out to eat at a restaurant. I spent ten minutes reading over every item on the menu, and couldn't decide what to order. For nearly ten years I'd never had a choice; I'd simply devoured whatever was plopped onto my plate. It seemed like an incredible luxury—and burden—to suddenly have to decide between roast beef, turkey, or ham entrée; baked potato, french fries, or rice pilaf; soup, tossed green salad, or cold slaw; and Coke, Pepsi, Seven-Up, Iced Tea, Milk, or half-a-dozen other beverages.

I also felt uncomfortable in casual conversations. Prison life was the only thing I seemed to know. When one of the boys' home instructors wanted to discuss politics or current events, I had nothing to contribute because I'd been isolated for so long. Fortunately, the kids only wanted to talk about prison life. They never tired of my stories. For that reason, I felt comfortable and at ease with them. I didn't have to pretend I was anything other than what I was—a dumb old ex-con.

One thing I had was lots of time to invest in the lives of the young boys, who came from all kinds of troubled backgrounds. Some didn't know their parents, or their parents had died; others had parents who either didn't love them or couldn't handle them. They were, for the most part, "problem" kids—tough and street-smart, and consequently difficult to manage. Nevertheless, like all children, they were fragile and needed to be handled with love. They'd already learned enough about hate and rejection and abandonment. What they needed was exactly what I had to give: time and love.

My job involved coaching all the athletic teams, counseling, and otherwise just spending time with the boys. The activity I enjoyed most was attending church with them each Sunday morning. We rode in an old blue-and-white bus that was rusted and rickety. But it still had enough working parts to transport a load of love-hungry kids to the nearby Baptist church in Orangeburg. The church was an imposing brick structure, but it was much more than just a building. It was a living, active, vibrant body of about five hundred people that welcomed our ragtag bunch into its arms. However, there were a few unanticipated adjustments I had to make as a paroled convict. In particular, I had to learn to control my behavior on Sunday mornings. In prison, there was a definite sense of worship in our chapel services, but we were free to clap, laugh, cry, hoot, and even belch when we felt like it. Now I had to appear more reserved. There was no belching allowed!

One of my most memorable Sundays was Mother's Day in 1978, shortly after my release from prison. It was special because I was thinking so much about my own mother. For the first time in ten years, I'd be spending Mother's Day with her. After the service, I planned to make the 170-mile drive to her home for dinner that night.

But the day was also special because the sermon struck deep roots with Toby, one of the boys who sat next to me. Toby was thirteen and disliked by most of the other kids because he was starving for attention. He'd have to rank among the greatest liars I ever met, but his fibbing was all done for attention. He managed to find many reasons to come up to my apartment, share a Pepsi, and just be together. Most often he would knock on my door, explaining that another adult had sent him to ask me a question: "Could I drive the bus the following Sunday?" "Did I lock up the basketball equipment after last weekend's game?" Of course, nobody had sent him. But I understood that, and I let him come in because I could see he just wanted to be loved.

Toby was all arms and legs, and absolutely pathetic on the athletic field. He tried to make up for it with big talk and bragging. The other kids resented his mouth and tried to pick fights, but he'd always back off when he was provoked. He was too gentle to be tough. There was a sweetness about him, and he was not afraid to say, "I love you," or "I care." He just needed somebody to love and care for him, too.

Most of all, Toby wanted a family to adopt him. He saw other orphans adopted, and wanted to know why they got more attention than he did. He couldn't understand why nobody would adopt him. Though he didn't realize it, his age was one strike against him, because most prospective adoptive parents wanted younger children. Several couples did take him to their homes to test his compatibility with their families. But they'd always bring him back for one reason or another. This caused him considerable anxiety and insecurity.

One day Toby told me that he never knew his father, and that his mother didn't care about him. "Why wouldn't they care about me?" he asked with tears in his eyes.

"I don't know your parents or why they gave you up," I responded. "But I doubt it had anything to do with you. Parents sometimes act very childish. They want a child, but later decide they can't be good parents."

Then I told him that I understood his hurt. "Toby, for nearly ten years I felt no one loved me. While I was in prison, I felt all alone and nobody really cared. But we have to realize Jesus has promised to never leave us or forsake us. Even though your parents disowned you, God never will. You have a father in Jesus, and He loves you—no matter what. He will always love you."

It hurt me as much as it did him that it was primarily the attractive kids who were invited to the homes of prospective adoptive parents. Every chance I got, I reinforced Christ's love for him, but I knew he needed something tangible. He needed skin. He needed arms around him, a body next to him. So one weekend, I told him, "Toby, I'm not letting anybody sign you out today. We're going to the beach at Pawleys Island. You're going to be my buddy this weekend. We're both outcasts; we don't need anybody, because we've got each other."

At the beach, Toby had the time of his life. I gave him money for rides and let him eat all the hot dogs and junk food he wanted. He acted like a boy turned loose in a toy store. After that weekend, he followed me everywhere. He wanted to be more special to me than the other kids, and was disturbed when I showed attention to others. Finally, I had to explain that even though he was my favorite, I couldn't deprive the other boys of my attention. That hurt him, as I knew it would. In the hurt in his eyes, I saw myself. In prison, I wanted just what he wanted—unlimited time and attention from one person. Unfortunately, no human being can give that to another. Only Jesus Christ can meet that need.

Toby professed to be a Christian, and accompanied me to church. And so he sat next to me in the fifth row that Mother's Day Sunday. The pastor presented awards and gifts to the oldest and youngest mothers in the congregation, and then preached about how mothers mirror God's love for us. In light of my reunion with my own mother, it was a very emotional message for me. She truly had revealed God's love to me when four years earlier—after I'd allowed no contact for five years—she said she loved me and was proud of me. I was like the prodigal son, returning home to a godly mother. Her devotion and thirty-four years of prayers paved the way for my meeting Christ.

As I looked around the church, I saw mothers sitting with children in their laps, and husbands with their arms draped proudly around the shoulders of their wives. Then I looked at the disadvantaged boys and couldn't help thinking how the pastor's message was being received by their little ears, because they had no mothers.

When the pastor gave an invitation at the end of the service, Toby got up and, without saying a word to me, walked down the aisle. I was surprised, and wondered what God was doing in his life. He looked so small and fragile in the large sanctuary, with his head bowed and the back of his dress shirt untucked from his Sunday slacks. His skinny frame looked like it would snap in the slightest breeze.

The pastor leaned over, and Toby whispered something in his ear. Then Toby turned around, and I could see his lips quivering and tears streaming down his face as he faced the congregation. With a shaking voice the pastor said, "Ladies and gentleman, little Toby from the boys' home has come to us with a very special prayer request. He hasn't seen his mother in more than five years, but he says he loves her very much and prays for her every day. Toby wants to know if we'll pray for his mother— that she's safe, and that one day she will love him."

As the pastor led in prayer, the entire congregation was gripped with emotion. When Toby came back and sat next to me, my eyes were flooded with tears. I leaned over, put my arm around his shoulders, and drew his body closer. "Toby, I can't take the place of your mother," I said, "but I love you and will be a father to you if you let me."

He put his hand on my leg and said, "I love you Mr. Morris."

I looked him in the eye. "I love you, too, son," I responded.

My relationship with Toby began to open my eyes to the deep hurts of people all around me. I had suffered nine-and-a-half years in prison for a murder I didn't commit, but compared to what many others have gone through, my suffering wasn't so bad. After all, I only got what I deserved. I had consorted with the scum of the earth and reaped what I'd sowed. But little Toby wasn't the cause of his own suffering. It wasn't his fault that his father and mother had deserted him. He needed love, and just as people had reached out and loved me, I could now reach out and love Toby and others like him.

Though I was very happy in the boys' home, I could not forget my prison roots. One week after my parole, I visited the local county jail in Orangeburg. One of the supporters of the home, Jimmy Frank, had a sideline prison ministry and invited me to tag along. "But don't tell anybody you've been in prison, or you won't get through the front gates," he warned me.

I didn't feel good about people not knowing who I was; I had nothing to hide. Nevertheless, I went along with this man with two first names, who when he wasn't speaking in prisons, was sitting under a tent on the street, passing out tracts.

Inside the jail, Jimmy set up an easel in the main dining area, which was surrounded by a circle of cells. Then he announced that there would be a brief service for those who wanted to come. Only three inmates emerged; the rest remained where they were, watching television or listening to their radios. Once the three men were seated, Jimmy pulled several large charts out of his briefcase, set them up on the easel, and with a pointer showed them the plan of salvation. The three men just sat there with blank expressions. One man looked at his neighbor and shrugged his shoulders. When it became obvious that these men were bored, I asked Jimmy if I could say something.

I looked the three men over slowly, and then said in a loud voice, "One week ago today I was released from Georgia State Penitentiary, where I spent nearly ten years of my life." As I started talking, the most amazing thing happened. One by one, televisions and radios were turned off, and the men emptied their cells. By the time I was finished, all but two of the inmates were listening. Jimmy Frank just sat there with his mouth agape. When I closed the time with prayer, several of the prisoners trusted Christ.

Shortly after that I was invited back to speak to the Lifer's Club at Georgia State Penitentiary. The group consisted of men who had served at least five years of a life sentence and were model inmates. The prison had a long-standing regulation that former inmates were not allowed back on the reservation. But after some discussion, Warden Thompson permitted me to enter, saying with a wink, "You're going to get me fired yet!"

After I addressed the Lifer's Club, the members gave me a standing ovation and voted unanimously to give me an honorary membership. They'd never done that before, and haven't since.

I made a number of visits to Georgia State Penitentiary in the following months. Bobby Richardson went with me on one of those occasions to speak at a special evening service. After the meeting, an old black inmate approached us. He had spent more than thirty years in prison, so we called him Slammer. There wasn't a dangerous bone in his body—he was just a thief. He was so accustomed to prison that whenever he was released, he'd promptly steal something and wind up right back behind bars. He liked the security of prison where he knew he was safe. There was no worry about rent money or what he'd wear, no light bills or car payments. This was the only life he could handle.

Though he was in his sixties, Slammer took good care of his body and had enjoyed knocking around with us on the basketball court. But I never realized what he thought of me until that night when he spoke to Bobby.

"Mr. Richardson, I want to tell you somethin' about Super Honky," he said, motioning at me with a jerk of his head. "The Honky was the best white player that ever come through here. This one day, we was out on the court, and Honky started talking to me. When we got done, he says, 'Slammer, you need what I got.' So I says, 'What you got, Honky?' So he tells me about the Lord. I don't say much back, but afterward go up to my cell, and I give my heart to Jesus just because of what the Honky said. Honky don't know that, but he led ol' Slammer to the Lord."

I was too choked up to say anything. His words made my prison years seem worthwhile. Slammer loved prison; for me it was a hell. Yet I'd been a witness to him, and didn't even know it. I wondered how many others God could touch through me now that I was free.

There were certainly plenty of hurting people around, and they didn't need my pity or sympathy. They needed love. Sometimes that love required drastic action. One day I learned about a teenage boy whose wealthy parents had disowned him. He had caused so much trouble that he'd been kicked out of every school in the county. He'd broken into a drugstore, stolen some drugs, and tried to overdose and kill himself. Paramedics managed to save him, and now he was in the local jail while the court decided what to do with him.

The next afternoon I visited the jail and asked to see the boy. He was the filthiest looking sight I had ever seen; you could smell him as soon as he entered the tiny visiting room. He wouldn't look me in the eye as I said, "Son, I want to ask you a question. When you broke into that store, were you trying to kill yourself, or did you just want some attention?"

He looked up at me and said, "Everybody is all hyped because they think I smoke marijuana. But I've been snorting cocaine since I was thirteen years old. You want to know why? I hate my dad! He gives me the money to buy drugs. He doesn't care about me. I'd kill him right now if I could get to him."

"Son, I want to tell you something," I said. "I don't know your father. And I don't know you, but I care about you very much. I'm going to arrange to have you turned over to me for twenty-four hours, and we're going to take a little trip to the Georgia State Penitentiary. I want you to meet some of my friends there, because if you continue your lifestyle, that's where you'll be living."

I made the proper arrangements and called Warden Thompson to ask if we could see three inmates. He agreed to cooperate and to call them in the order I requested. The boy and I arrived, and the warden accompanied us with two guards to a secure room. The first man called down was Horse, whose body was solid as its namesake, and whose face resembled the south end of a horse heading north. He had been in the penitentiary for nineteen years. It was a hot, unbearably humid South Georgia day, yet Horse wore a sweat shirt. That was just the first layer. He wore a shirt over that, plus a prison jacket. A scarf was knotted around his neck, and a prison hat was pulled so low that the rim nearly touched his dark glasses.

Horse walked up to the boy. "Hey kid, what's your name?" he demanded.

The boy just about forgot his name. "Mm . . . Mm . . . Mmmalcolm, sir."

"Boy, how old are you?"

"Ssseventeen, sir."

"When I was your age, I was jailed for murder. I robbed a

bank. I rented a motel and filled it up with women. Then I came here and killed three teenagers just like you, boy." He reached into his pocket and pulled out three indictments that he'd carried around for nineteen years. "Get over here and look at these," he commanded, unfolding the paper. Malcolm took a hesitant step closer. "I said get over here, boy. I don't bite." Malcolm eased another step closer. "Get off my foot!" Horse suddenly yelled.

"Yes, sir!" Malcolm jumped back, though he wasn't even on his foot.

After Horse left, Warden Thompson called down the next inmate. He was known as Monkey Man because his back was covered with hair. Though only thirty-seven years old, he looked much older. He sat in front of Malcolm and said, "Son, I care about you very much. Let me tell you about my life. You see, at age ten I killed my mother. Beat her to death with a baseball bat. I've been here twelve years. I also have two life sentences for rape. I deserve to die in prison. I never received a letter, and I probably never will. The only friend I have in the world is Harold. Because of him, I've turned my life around and know Jesus Christ as my personal Savior."

"Son, you don't want this kind of life, believe me. I want you to leave here today, and I want you to listen to Harold. He cares about you. Please, no alcohol or drugs. No illicit sex. Son, I'd do anything on earth to keep you from living the kind of life I've had to live." Then he got up and walked out.

I'd saved the best for last. His name was Big Mac. He'd been in prison for twenty-four years. He weighed 250 pounds and had tattoos and stab wounds all over his body. He was a drug addict, a homosexual, and one of the most violent men I'd ever known.

Big Mac strode into the room, grabbed Malcolm, and lifted him off the floor. "Punk, what's your name?" he demanded.

This time, Malcolm completely forgot his name.

Big Mac glanced at me, and then said to Malcolm, "Listen to me. I don't like Morris. I never have. He's a Jesus Freak, so ignore what he says. When you leave here today, I want you to go out and smoke dope. I want you to rob, steal, murder. Do it all, son, because then you'll come back here, and I'll make you my boy. You're cute. And when I get hold of you, I ain't never gonna let you get out of prison." Then he pulled the boy toward him and kissed him hard on the lips.

"Let me out!" he screamed as Big Mac eased his grip. "Let me out!" All but Malcomb were laughing as we opened the door. The boy promptly dashed to the parking lot and scrambled into the car. When I finally joined him, he didn't say anything. After we'd been on the highway for a few minutes, he looked over at me, and I saw he was crying. "Mr. Morris, will you help me?" he asked.

"What do you want me to do?"

"Mr. Morris, I would take my life right now if I knew I had to go to that prison. I can't live there. That man who killed three teenagers—he's proud of it! The other man killed his mother, and that man who kissed me. . . . Please help me. I'll do anything."

"Do you really mean that?"

"Yes. I'm ready to change."

The next day I talked to Malcolm's family and the judge, and arranged for his probation. Malcolm agreed to be tested for drugs once a week. We managed to get him back into school, and he settled down and eventually graduated.

At the boys' home, I found many opportunities to exercise such tough love. I maintained an open door policy with the boys that they could stop by my apartment any time to talk about anything. They also knew whatever they shared would be kept in confidence.

Roy, a fourteen-year-old, knocked on my door one night, and I invited him in for a soft drink. Roy was just the opposite of Toby. He was a tough, athletic kid with dark hair and a handsome face. He was intelligent, and I found it easy to communicate with him.

"What's on your mind?" I asked.

"Mr. Morris, I'm going to run away," Roy said. "I know you won't tell on me. You always said that if I had a problem, I could tell you about it, and you wouldn't turn me in."

"No, I won't turn you in," I assured him. "But will you tell me why you want to run away?"

"This boys' home is a prison, and I'm tired of it. I think I can do better on the outside."

"How are you going to get to where you want to go?"

"I'll thumb rides."

"Fine, but you've picked a bad day. It's starting to rain. It's late in the afternoon, and soon it'll be dark. Thumbing rides is dangerous. I'm sure you've heard stories about young male hitch-hikers being kidnapped and robbed. I mean, that's something to think about, although I'm sure you already have. I won't try to influence you; the decision is yours."

He leaned back thoughtfully on my couch.

"How much money do you have?" I asked.

"A couple bucks."

"I don't know if you can wait this long, but I'm speaking at a sports banquet Friday night, and I'd really like for you to go with me. You could sit at the head table with me, and have a good meal."

"Well . . ."

"Roy, you're a great young athlete, and you probably have more ability at your age than any of the boys who will be receiving awards at that dinner. Someday you can be honored just like them. I'd like you to see what it's all about, and you might decide you want to be a great athlete."

"You honestly think that, Mr. Morris?"

"Honest."

"Then maybe I'll wait until after the weekend to run away. I'll stick around and go with you."

On the way home from the banquet later that week, Roy said, "You know Mr. Morris, I'm better than any of those guys. I want to go to high school and be a good athlete. Do you think I could?"

"I *know* you could," I said.

Roy stayed at the boys' home, went to high school, and eventually did quite well as an athlete. But that didn't just happen. He needed adults who would stand behind him and believe that kids are worth any price and inconvenience. He needed adults who would love him and offer him understanding and guidance. In Roy's case, I happened to be one of those individuals.

I know there are thousands of others just like Toby, Malcolm and Roy who are on the lookout for love. To give that love requires faith. And that's not as easy as it sounds. Tough faith means being tender and understanding, confronting when necessary, and expressing belief that each of these youngsters has some under-lying ability that he can tap. Each boy in that home was important. He was worthwhile. God had made him for a reason.

There were some more lessons about tough faith that I would learn in the boys' home, and also in other settings, particularly at a campground in Myrtle Beach.

Chapter Five

HARD LESSONS

Three months after my release from prison, I made the three-hour drive to Myrtle Beach taking one of the kids from the boys' home with me. While I was there, the chaplain of a campground asked me to speak at a Sunday morning church service. There on a beautiful July day, a thousand people, most of them in bathing trunks and shorts, gathered for the outdoor meeting. It was an idyllic setting, with the Atlantic rolling up on the beach directly behind me.

After I gave my testimony and an invitation, several people approached me to talk. While interacting with them, I noticed a woman standing off to one side. She had on white shorts, an ocean-blue top, and a turban covering most of her shortish blond hair. Tears were streaming down her face, and she wore the most pitiful expression I've ever seen. Immediately I excused myself from the crowd and went over to her.

"Ma'am, can I help you?" I asked.

The woman's lips were trembling but I managed to understand most of what she said. "How . . . how can you stand up there and talk about God . . . and how He's blessed you?. . . How can you talk about faith after what you've gone through?"

Gently I escorted her to one of the benches, and we sat down. "Ma'am, I don't know how to answer that. But if you'd like, I'd be glad to listen if you need to talk."

She started crying harder, and I was at a loss to know what to do. "Please, come with me," I said. I led her to the chaplain's office, a small room next to the amphitheater where I'd talked. There, I learned her name was Becky Smith. Taking a deep breath, she began to speak. "Seven months ago, my husband and son were killed in a plane crash." With those words, she choked up and couldn't talk for a few moments. I felt awkward and uneasy. Here I was, fresh out of prison, trying to help someone who was hurting far more than I ever had. Prison was a piece of cake compared to her suffering. I had no idea what to say or do.

Since I had the youngster from the boys' home with me, I decided to use him as an excuse to buy some time. "Are you camping here at Myrtle Beach?" I finally asked as she wiped her eyes.

"My daughter and I have been here two weeks," she responded weakly.

"Then could I come back tomorrow without the boy, so we could talk more?"

She agreed to meet me at the chaplain's office the next morning at eleven o'clock. I was glad to have a day to think about the situation. My experience in prison and in the boys' home was showing me that I was somehow supposed to help hurting people. While I knew prisoners and was comfortable with teenage boys, I was at a loss to know how to deal with this woman. Yet I felt I could not leave her alone. Someone had to help her, and apparently that person was me. God would have to show me what to do.

The next day, one of my brothers agreed to look after the boy while I went to my appointment. This time Becky was more stable, but just barely. With a faraway look in her eyes, she began to tell me her story. Earlier that year, Becky and her family had gone to Florida to be with her husband's parents for Christmas. On December 27, her husband, twelve-year-old son and two other relatives went flying in a small four-seat airplane. The plane had crashed in a field near his parents' house, killing everyone on board. "How could God allow this to happen?" she asked, wiping her eyes.

"I don't know," I answered. "I don't know. I don't have the answers. But I *can* say I care."

It had been seven months since the tragedy and I was curious what had brought Becky to Myrtle Beach. "My daughter, Tonya, wanted to come here to camp," she explained. "Every summer, our whole family had spent three weeks here, and she wanted to return because she has so many happy memories of our times here." Becky started weeping again. "It's been so hard . . . I didn't want to come, but I did for her because she needed it. . . . It's been very, very painful for me. These past two weeks, I've been surrounded by families. And here we are alone, just the two of us. . . . We go sit on the beach, and thousands of people walk by. But nobody cares."

"I care," I said, squeezing her arm lightly.

"I know that. I don't know why I came to hear you yesterday, though. I'm so angry at God, I just haven't wanted to go to church. But yesterday morning I thought, *I need to be in church.* I sat in the last row, and as you talked I gripped my seat. I thought, *Here is a man who is talking about faith in God, and he has suffered. Maybe he would care.*"

"That's why you came down?"

She nodded.

"I hope you don't mind me asking this. But I need to know if you've ever asked Jesus Christ to come into your life."

"Yes, at fourteen. In fact, I can't ever remember not being a Christian. But . . ." She paused, and I knew she was trying to say she felt her faith was dead. "I just don't have it anymore. I loved my husband and son more than anything. We had a great marriage and a very special family. We had good jobs. He was a band director; I was a school teacher. I felt our lives were making a difference. Everything was going our way . . . until the crash. Why would God cut my family in half? How could He destroy my life?" She was sobbing now. I have no reason to live. Tell me, why should I live?"

At this point I didn't think she needed me to read a lot of Scripture or try to manufacture a three-point answer. What she needed was someone to listen, to weep with her, to try to understand how she was feeling, to provide strong arms to hold her and a gentle voice to share Christian love.

"I've gone through a lot myself, though nothing like what you're going through," I said, hoping to encourage her. "All I can say is that Jesus is the answer, and He saved me. He got me out of prison, and He's the reason I'm here today. I owe Him everything.

"I wish I knew why I went to prison," I continued. "I wish I knew why we suffer. I wish I knew why you lost your husband and son. I would do anything on earth if I could bring them back. But I can't. I don't know what to say to you except that I love you as a Christian and God loves you and will help you. Please, trust Him, Becky."

"How can you talk about faith and God's love?" she protested. "How can you believe in God after spending ten years in prison for a crime you didn't commit?!"

"I guess I can't explain it to you," I said. "I just know He's all I've got. And I know He freed me."

There was nothing else to say. I could only cry with Becky and let her know that if she wanted to talk further, I was available. We were together for about an hour when she stood to leave. I put my arms around her shoulders and said, "I want you to know I'll do anything in the world to help you and your daughter. I'm going back to Orangeburg tomorrow. You can call me. But please, don't take your life. When you think about suicide, call me and talk to me. I'll be there, and we'll try to work it out together."

The next day I drove back to the boys' home, sobered by my contact with Becky. A few days later, I received a short note from her, thanking me for our time together. A week after that, I called her in Hendersonville, North Carolina. She was shocked when I told her who was calling. "How did you get my phone number?" she asked.

"Ex-cons have connections," I said with a laugh. We began talking by phone almost every week. I was glad to provide a strong shoulder to cry on and be a much-needed sounding board for her.

Meanwhile, my work at the boys' home continued. It was an adventure, and I never knew what I'd face on any given day. In the gymnasium one afternoon, two of the boys, Lee and Dave, disrupted basketball practice with yelling and cursing. I blew the whistle, and told them to step off the court.

"Dave hit me in the face," Lee yelled, to which Dave responded with a string of expletives.

"Get over here, both of you," I ordered.

Lee was a red-haired, freckle-faced, fourteen-year-old with a wiry body that hadn't filled out yet. He was our best athlete, with the natural talent to become a top performer. But he didn't have the right attitude; he'd never been coached and wasn't raised in a supportive home. Dave was a tousle-haired street kid who was found one day eating out of a garbage can. He was clumsy and non-athletic, but compensated for his lack of ability with a big mouth. At fifteen, he was a natural hothead who liberally spewed profanity. Because Dave couldn't compete fairly with kids his own age, he loved to beat up the little boys and then laugh about it.

"I want to apologize to you," I said, eyeballing both youngsters. "I forgot to tell you that there's something I love even more than basketball, and that's watching a good brawl. Anytime you want to fight, all you have to do is tell me, and we'll stop practice so you can go at each other. You two have been arguing and pushing and shoving all day. So I'm going to let you slug it out. When you're finished, I'll take the loser to the hospital, have him stitched up, and then we'll continue practice."

Neither boy said a word as they stared at their shoes.

"Did you understand me?" I asked.

"But I don't want to fight," Dave grumbled.

"What do you mean? You've already disrupted practice and showed no respect for any of us. So you either fight or get out of this gymnasium for one week. The decision's yours. Fight or get out. Now."

With heads still lowered, they turned and walked out. After that, an unbelievable thing happened. Behavior improved remarkably. When boys started pushing or shoving during practice, I'd blow my whistle and say, "Does anybody want to fight?"

"No, sir," they always insisted. They were even careful not to foul each other, lest it appear they were fighting. They knew I meant what I said.

Incidents such as these convinced me more than ever that kids were worth saving, no matter what the price. Part of that price was consistent discipline. They needed to know exactly what was expected, and that there were guaranteed consequences if they refused to heed the rules. Along with that discipline came constant affirmation. Those boys knew I loved them because I told them every day, and because I wouldn't let them get away with behavior that I knew, if not corrected, would eventually destroy their lives.

Birthdays at the boys' home were always special to me. I'd take the boys out to eat and treat them to a movie or bowling. One of the boys was especially excited about going to his favorite restaurant for his birthday. Hal was a sandy-haired fourteen-year-old who made excellent grades, got along well with other kids, and always seemed happy. He was on a natural high, and kept a perpetually good attitude. On the basketball court, he was a good little athlete who quickly learned everything I tried to teach him. But he blew it all one afternoon, on his birthday.

That day, Hal talked back to me during basketball practice, and used profanity in front of the other kids. I ordered him to leave the gym, which he did. After practice I was walking across the yard toward my apartment when Hal ran up to me.

"How's everything going?" he began formally.

"I'm doing fine, and you?"

"Not so well. I want to ask you something, Mr. Morris. Do you accept apologies?"

"I sure do. Do you want to apologize about something?"

"Yes, sir. I'm really sorry about the way I acted today. I was wrong."

"I accept your apology, son. It takes a man to apologize, and I'm proud of you."

When I started to walk on, he said, "Are we still going to dinner at six?"

"No, we aren't going, son."

"What do you mean?" Tears began to form in his eyes. It's my birthday, and you said you forgave me."

"I do forgive you, and as far as I'm concerned it's a dead issue. I'll never again hold it against you. But you must learn to show respect to others. You didn't show respect, so you must be punished. I'm sorry, but that's my decision."

He dropped his head and turned away. Later, as I walked to the chow hall for dinner, I decided that if Hal came in acting as if nothing happened, then I would take him out. It would signal that he had learned his lesson, and we would celebrate as planned. However, if he was sullen I'd know he really didn't mean that apology, and that he needed further discipline. Naturally I hoped he would be the same old, fun-loving Hal. A few moments later, he showed up and sat down next to me as he usually did.

"Hey, man, why are you eating that slop?" I asked him.

"What do you mean?"

"I mean we're going to town and eat a steak!"

"Whoopie!" he yelled, jumping up to hug me.

After that, Hal was more respectful, and I never had another discipline problem with him. Of course, you don't win them all, and I had my share of failures—the most painful involving a blond-haired, blue-eyed boy named Danny. He was nine years old, and was everything I could ever hope for in a son. If boys are made out of snips, snails and puppy dog tails, little Danny got double of everything. I'd never seen a kid as competitive and tough at his age. He'd fight if necessary, yet he knew how to laugh. He said hip things, walked with a swagger, was built solid as a pit bull terrier, and had confidence that wouldn't quit. He had a smart little mouth, and when I'd call "Danny!" he'd answer, "That's my name, don't wear it out." Perhaps because he reminded me of myself at his age, I loved him more than all the other boys. I would have given anything to raise him as my son, love him, educate him, and teach him in the ways of the Lord.

Endurance was another quality I appreciated, and Danny would never quit. One day I read in the paper about a track meet in Columbia, South Carolina, for outstanding state athletes aged nine through seventeen. The top three finishers in each event would be eligible to enter the National Junior Olympics.

The boys at the home had never competed in a track meet, so

I made special arrangements for them to participate in these races. I explained the events to the kids and coached them for a week. On Saturday morning, we hopped into an old van and drove forty miles to Columbia. On the way over we had a word of prayer, and then I gave them a little speech.

"If you enter an event, you must finish," I said. "That's all I ask of you. I don't expect you to win, but I do expect you to compete to the best of your ability and cross the finish line. The kids you're competing against are well-trained; they're the best in the state. They're already winners, or they wouldn't be here. But, you've been allowed to compete, and you wanted to go. So no half-efforts. You finish, and I promise that after the meet I'll feed you all the hamburgers you can eat."

Several thousand people were there to watch the track and field events. All ten kids I brought finished their events, though some of them walked across the finish line. It was pitiful looking at some of them, the way they were dressed. They were anything but athletes, and people laughed at them. I ignored the laughs and worked on the infield, coaching the boys and giving them Pepsi Colas and hot dogs to keep their spirits up.

The last event of the day was the mile run, in which Danny was competing. None of the boys had won any awards, but I felt Danny had a chance. There were twenty other competitors in that race; two of whom were rated as the top runners in the state. One owned the state record for his age group. As Danny headed for the starting line, I told him, "All you've got to do is finish third. You'll get a medal and qualify for the National Junior Olympics. Now listen to me. It's hot, and you must run four laps around this track. I'll stay near you here on the infield and help you pace yourself. Just listen to me."

The gun sounded, and Danny quickly took the lead and held it through the second lap. The two top runners caught him, and racing as a trio they lapped the other athletes by the final round. The boy that held the state record took a one-hundred yard lead and finished first. Danny and the other top runner were neck and neck at the finish line, but Danny took second by a breath.

I ran to the finish line, whooping like a wild Indian, and grabbed

Danny. I lifted him up on my shoulders and ran him around the track. This was more fun than all the athletic awards I'd won in high school! Danny, an untrained, uncoached castoff, had finished second! I was crying with joy as I looked up and saw his blond hair waving in the air and his smile about ready to burst.

When Danny accepted his medal, he took one look at the prize and turned to me. "One day I'll win the Olympic gold medal," he said brightly. Since he'd qualified for the National Junior Olympics, I suggested that we register immediately. "I'll pay your fee," I said.

He shook his head. "I can't enter."

"What do you mean?" I said.

"I don't want to be away from the home. My mother might come to get me, and I have to be there."

I loved Danny so much and wanted to do whatever I could to help him develop his potential. And I wanted to spare him the heartache of holding onto a dream that I was certain would never come true. Danny's mother had given him up several years before, and I'd never heard of a mother reclaiming her child after that long.

What I really wanted to do was adopt him, but I was prevented from doing that because I'd been to prison and was unmarried. So I figured out an alternative. I went to my brother in Pawleys Island, South Carolina, and explained the situation. He agreed to adopt him, but when I discussed the plan with Danny he objected. "My mother might come back," he said.

I was disappointed he would pass up the advantages a stable family could offer him. Not wanting to concede defeat to a nine-year-old-boy, I invited him to spend a week with my brother's family that summer. My brother had a son two years older than Danny, and together the youngsters had a great time. On the drive back to the boys' home, I asked Danny what he thought of my family.

"They're cool."

"Do you like my nephew?"

"He's a little mean, but I straightened him out."

"Well, how would you like to live with them?"

"No thanks."

"But you just said you liked them. They'd be good to you."

"I tried a family once, and I'll never do that again. Nobody cares."

"Listen to me, son. I care. And I'd like to adopt you. You could stay with my brother for now. Once I get married, you can come live with me, and I'll love and educate you. My family will support and stand by you. You can count on me. I'll be loyal to you. I'll give you the life you've never known. I really love you."

Then, without thinking about the potential consequences of what I was saying, I added, "I know this is hard for you to accept, but your mother is never coming back to get you. She doesn't care, or else she'd have returned by now. You've got to give up that dream, son."

Danny looked at me with sudden fury in his eyes. "I hate you!" he sputtered. "You're just like all the others. You call yourself a Christian, but you don't care! You don't love me! You don't understand! My mother cares about me. She had to make a decision about keeping me or my baby sister, and she gave me away. But she loves me, and one day she's coming back."

"Son, I'm sorry. I didn't mean . . ."

"I hate you," he yelled.

"Son, I'm sorry, I'm sorry," I said, with tears in my eyes. I'd have given anything if I could have taken back those words, but Danny never forgave me. From that point until the day I left the home, he hardly said ten words to me. No matter what I tried to do, he refused my friendship.

My impulsive response ruined our relationship. But I learned a significant truth: No one can take the place of parents in a child's heart. No matter what happens, a child loves his parents and wants to be loved by them. I should have remembered that from my own experience.

Though I ruined our friendship, I had the joy of knowing that before our falling out I had led him to Christ. Danny was among the boys who accompanied me to church and to some of my speaking engagements. I'd sit them in the front row, but I never tried to force anything on them. Over a period of time, I could see the seed of faith had been planted, and on the way back from church one Sunday, I asked Danny if he'd thought any more about making a decision to trust Christ.

"Yeah, I've thought about it," he said.

"Would you like to pray with me today?" I asked.

"Yeah, Mr. Morris, I would. How about now?"

So right there, driving down the interstate in my sky-blue Monte Carlo, we prayed together, and Danny invited Jesus into his heart. When we arrived back at the boys' home, I shut off the engine and turned to face him. "When you trust Christ, that means you're going to change. You've got to be a leader out here, Danny, because all these kids look up to you."

"I understand, Mr. Morris," he said.

"You know, you've been kind of hard on some of them. You'll need to take things a little easier. Of course, Jesus will help you. He doesn't expect you to change on your own. And I'll be there to help you, too. You can talk to me anytime."

"Yeah, I know."

"Now, you need to go tell all the other kids what you've done. It's important they know you're a Christian now. They'll be glad to know they won't get beat up anymore."

Danny laughed, opened the door, and took off flying.

Most of the youngsters at the home professed to be Christians. They'd tell you they'd been saved. But most didn't understand what that meant. They would go to church, and many of them would go forward every Sunday. After one service, a boy who'd walked down the aisle during the invitation told me he'd been saved three times before. It felt so good he wanted to get saved again. That was his way of getting love and attention. But Danny was different. With him, I believe it was real. He was the kind of guy who, when he made a commitment, didn't back down— just as he didn't back down when I insulted him about his mother.

Later, when I visited the boys' home during a break from Bible college, I was surprised to learn that Danny's mother finally did return for him. His daddy, whom he never knew, had been killed in a motorcycle accident. There was a will, and his mother needed the boy to collect some insurance money. So she came and got him, and they moved to Texas. After several years I found out he'd dropped out of school and was hanging out on the street. Knowing his toughness, I figured that would happen. It would have been impossible for him to have stayed out of trouble in that environment without Christian support. It breaks my heart to think he could be in prison now, especially knowing I could have given him the support he needed to make it. I'd love to see him again; I hate to think I might have to visit a prison to do that.

One day, two boys at the home, aged sixteen and seventeen, broke into the director's office and stole some money. Charges were filed, and they were eventually sent off to a reformatory. The night before they left, I went over to witness to them and tell them I still loved them. But they rejected that, and one of them spit at me. "You're just blowing smoke, Morris," he said. "Like everybody else, you don't give a rip about us. I'll go to prison and die there. Who cares? My daddy and mamma don't care. Nobody cares."

Several months passed, and then one day I got a letter from the boy who'd spit at me. "Mr. Morris, I want to apologize for the things I said to you," he wrote. "You really do care, and I know you love me. I wouldn't listen to you when you told me about prison, and I disregarded everything I saw and heard when you took me to visit your old friends at Georgia State Penitentiary. It's too late for me, but I now remember the things you said. If only I had one more chance. . . ."

I jumped in my car, drove to the reformatory, and led that boy to Christ. Several months later, he was released and returned to the boys' home. He was changed, because he'd had a personal encounter with Jesus Christ. That showed me again how nothing can take the place of leading a young boy to Christ, and then discipling him so he grows up to be a man of God. I thank God I had the opportunity to help some youngsters break through the barriers of their upbringing and discover that God gives them another chance. Those youngsters were my own sons, and I knew my faith would never be the same because of them.

But God had more in store for me than the boys' home. One of the major reasons for my Christian growth after prison was being able to attend Harmony Church. Bobby Richardson was an elder in the church, and prior to my parole he had heard me speak. He promptly told his pastor, Bob Norris, that he ought to schedule me for a Sunday service. So a date was set for April 3rd. There was only one problem: Bobby forgot to tell his pastor I was still in prison.

When the church later discovered I was jailed with two life sentences and couldn't come unless I busted out, the members could easily have scratched my name off the calendar and scheduled someone else. Instead, they prayed that I'd be able to keep the date. I like to believe their prayers were one major reason I was paroled March 14th and was able to speak at Harmony Church as scheduled.

The members of that little church were an important encouragement to me. They called me on the phone, opened their homes, loved me when I felt unlovable, and helped me learn God's Word. At that time Bobby Richardson and Pastor Norris frequently reminded me, "Harold, any wrong move you make right now will come back to haunt you. Spend time with us and work on your testimony. God has great plans for you."

Those two men discipled me and gave me opportunities to speak. However, they became convinced I needed more training than they could provide. "Preparation before performance" was my motto in prison, and they suggested I enroll in a Bible college to become more grounded in Scripture. I wasn't at all thrilled with the idea. After all, I was twice the age of most students. But out of respect for these men, I applied to a Bible college.

During these months, I continued to correspond with Becky and talk with her by phone. Late one night, her call got me out of bed. She was deeply depressed and said several times, "There's no reason for me to live. I can't go on."

"I'm coming up to see you," I said. "Just hold on. I'll be there by noon tomorrow."

The next morning, I hopped in my car and drove to

Hendersonville, North Carolina, about a four-hour drive. "We're going for a picnic in the park," I said, and so we did.

The serene park setting, with a gentle breeze in the trees and birds singing, seemed to have a calming effect on Becky. She obviously needed to talk, so I listened.

"There's an airport near our house," she said. "For five months, I couldn't even bear to drive by because it reminded me of the crash. Oh Harold, it still hurts so much. Just last week, I had to go to a band festival that was being dedicated to my husband. As I sat there watching his band, I cried out in the middle of all those people, "God, I hate you! I hate you! I hate you! . . .""

I was crying with her as I said, "That's okay. God knows you're hurting. He understands."

She tried to smile. "Deep down, very deep, I think so, too," she said, and then launched into a story about a young boy who used to be in her class.

"One day during recess, he was creating problems with the other children, but when I asked him to stop, he wouldn't. So I picked him up in my arms, and he started kicking and screaming. The more he kicked and yelled, the tighter I held him. I told him, 'Kent, I'm not putting you down until you stop.' I carried him away from the other children, sat with him on the school steps and just held him. After a little while, I felt the fight go out of him, and he just went to sleep."

Becky shook her head as she thought about it. "That's how it is with God and me right now. I kick and scream and cry, and He just holds me."

"Many times in prison I was so discouraged and lonely," I said. "I was ready to give up all hope. But as miserable as I was, I never lost the joy that comes from knowing Christ as my Lord and Savior."

"Joy? I don't feel much of that right now. The only thing that keeps me going are friends like you. Now and then I see a little improvement, but I need time to heal."

"Well, we've got time," I said with a smile. "I'm here to help hold you up. There were friends who held me up while I was in prison, and who helped me make the adjustment when I got out."

When I asked Becky how her daughter was doing, she said Tonya was still having nightmares. "She and her daddy were very close," she added, looking far off toward the horizon.

"I hope I can meet her sometime," I said.

Becky glanced at her watch. "How about right now!" she said. "She's with some friends, and I need to pick her up."

Tonya was an adorable, nine-year-old girl with red hair, freckles, and a bubbling personality. Almost immediately she gave me a big hug. That afternoon, I took them out for ice cream and told them some corny jokes. "Did you hear the one about the green bean and the pea? They were walking down the road and a reckless driver ran over the little green bean. Well, they called the ambulance and rushed it to the hospital. The little pea was out in the waiting room, worried to death about his little friend. Finally the doctor came out and said, 'Mr. Pea, I have good news and bad news.' The pea said, 'Please, give me the good news first.' The doctor said, 'Well, the good news is your little friend will live. The bad news is he will be a vegetable the rest of his life.'"

Tonya screamed at that and hugged me. "Tell me another!" she said.

"What do you call an alligator on welfare?" I asked.

She shrugged.

"Gator Aid!"

Again she howled with laughter. "Gator Aid! I love it." Becky was also laughing hard, and I could see the heavy weight on her lift just a little. It felt good to be able to bring some cheer to this hurting family.

As I left to drive back to the boys' home, I hugged Becky and Tonya and told them I loved them. Tonya practically choked me with her arms, and my heart went out to her. She had so much love to give, and I wanted to love her as though she were my own daughter. As for Becky, I loved her as a special friend. It wasn't romance; she wasn't ready for that kind of relationship anyway. But she needed some strong arms of support, and I was willing to provide them. If Becky and Tonya needed to lean on me for awhile, that was fine with me.

And so I began to learn what true love was. God's love. His love accepted people where they were hurting. It took young boys who had been rejected by their parents and gave them a strong father figure they needed. It took a young girl whose father had died and showed her how to laugh. It took a deeply hurting woman, and provided a listening ear and a supportive arm. Through His Holy Spirit, God was teaching me how to love His way.

Chapter Six

THE JOY OF GIVING

To learn more about God's ways, I knew I needed to attend Bible college. But when I first approached my parole officer with the idea, I hit an immovable barrier.

"I'm sorry, Harold, rules are rules," she said. "You must stay in the state."

When my first application to another Bible school in state was rejected earlier, I interpreted it as God's signal that college just wasn't for me. Bob Norris saw differently. He went ahead and arranged for me to attend Southeastern Bible College in Birmingham, Alabama. There was only one condition. The semester had already started, so I would have to report in two days. However, my parole officer wouldn't budge.

"You've got to understand, Harold, that I'm just following the law," she explained for at least the fifth time. "I'm not making the decision. The guidelines have been set by the state."

"Yes, ma'am," I said sullenly.

"An official variance from the state would take months to get approved, and you want to leave tomorrow?"

"Yes, ma'am."

"There's a mountain of paperwork that has to be filled out and approved by everybody from the Pope on down. All the forms have to be sent to Georgia, then to Alabama. That takes time."

"Yes, ma'am."

"This is Friday, and offices close in a couple of hours. Nothing can happen today, and like I said, I don't think I can get an answer for several months. You've got to understand."

"I'm trying hard, ma'am." I cleared my throat and looked her in the eyes. "I understand everything you've said, and I understand that the law is the law. What I don't understand is why it's so difficult for an ex-con to do something with his life, to serve God, to study the Word of God. I want you to explain that to me."

She looked at me without saying a word.

"Without your approval, I can't attend Bible college. I understand why you're saying no. But there's an awful lot of people who are praying you will say yes."

"Harold, you're not—"

"Let me talk for a minute," I interrupted. "How would I be hurting anybody? How much trouble can I get into at Bible school? You'd know exactly where I was, and could check on me anytime. I'd think everybody would be glad for a convict to study the Word of God. I mean, one school turned me down, which was fine with me. But now I'm prepared to go."

"Harold, you—"

"By parole rules, I can get a job doing anything. I could tell you tomorrow I want to change jobs and dig ditches, and you'd say, 'Great!' But you won't let me go to Bible school, and . . . well, I guess I *don't* understand."

Deep in thought, she looked away for a long moment. Then she let out a sigh, threw up her hands, and scribbled something on a slip of paper. Turning back to me, she said, "Here, take this travel pass, and if you get stopped in transit, have the authorities call me. I'm putting my job on the line. But you go, and you study the Word of God."

"Thank you," I said, as my eyes brimmed with tears. "Thank you, thank you, thank you."

"You'll need to report to a parole officer when you arrive," she said, handing me another sheet of paper with the proper officer's name and address. "He should phone me Monday morning, but by then I'll have the paperwork moving."

"I don't know what else to say, other than I hope I'll someday be able to return the favor." Then I embraced her warmly and left, knowing that faith had just moved a mountain.

Unlike other students who were half my age, I did not receive tuition money from my parents every term. In fact, most of my family thought I was crazy going back to school. I didn't want to assume God would somehow arrange for mysterious envelopes stuffed with cash to be deposited in my bank account. So I began accepting weekend speaking engagements at nearby churches. I never charged, but the churches would often take up love offerings to help me. God also moved many people to help me along the way with unsolicited but timely contributions of a few dollars to a thousand dollars or more. In this way, I was able to pay my bills over the next three years.

School was a tremendous adjustment, especially first term when I carried a load of twenty-one semester hours. It took awhile to get used to the discipline, and more than once I felt like quitting. One night I called Becky to get a morale boost. "Guess what," I told her. "I'm in Bible school."

"That's great!" she said.

"I'm not so sure. I'm having a hard time getting used to studying."

"If I know one thing about you, you're not a quitter. I know you can do it."

Her encouragement was a tremendous lift to me. We talked to each other on the phone frequently. When she was depressed, we might talk for an hour or longer until her spirits lifted. Many times, Tonya would join our conversation, and usually she would ask me to repeat some of my corny jokes. "Tell me about Gator Aid," she'd say. That was her favorite.

There was no doubt by now that Becky and I were attracted to each other. But when we talked about it, I candidly told her, "I have nothing to offer you. I'm forty years old, with no job and no money. I'm struggling in school and don't know if I can cut it in the ministry. You don't want me; I'd just fail you. God's got someone much better for you."

Becky didn't know all about the deep insecurity swirling inside me. It dated back to my disastrous marriage before prison, long before I had a relationship with Christ. I, the superstar athlete, had married the high school beauty queen, an intelligent woman with convictions and goals for college and career. She was much too good for me. I had rested on my athletic laurels and spent my free time chasing around. Katie did her best to make the marriage work, but I sabotaged her efforts and finally left her. Even as she secured the divorce, I knew I'd made a terrible mistake. I told her, "Someday, you'll realize that getting rid of me was the best thing that ever happened to you."

More than nine years in prison further complicated my thoughts concerning marriage. During my incarceration, I dealt exclusively with men. Women were thought of only as sex objects. I'd forgotten they were real people; that they had needs, feelings, drives, and emotions as strong as my own. Because of that, I had no confidence I could ever communicate adequately with a woman; surely I'd fall short of her expectations of what a husband should be. I knew ex-convicts often married quickly after their release. But those marriages invariably ended in divorce, and I didn't want to add another failure to my life. So I kept my distance, and didn't allow the relationship to get serious.

I was still convinced that Becky needed caring Christian support, without any romantic pressure. Soon after I enrolled in Bible college, Bobby Richardson and his family moved to Ashville, North Carolina, just thirty miles from Becky's home. I told Betsy, Bobby's wife, about Becky. Betsy is a wonderful Christian lady who frequently speaks to Christian women's clubs, and is also a good counselor. "Would you do me a favor?" I asked her. I explained my relationship with Becky, and then said, "I think she really needs some strong female support right now. Would you spend some time with her?"

I also told Bobby about Tonya, and how she didn't have a father. Bobby and Betsy followed through, invited them to their home, and became friends. It meant a great deal to know there were people like the Richardsons who, on the basis of a phone call, were willing to reach out and help my friends, no strings attached.

At school, one of the highlights of every week was Monday

night when I took a group of students with me to a nearby all-you-can-eat restaurant. At first, I invited one or two individuals, but the group quickly grew to about fifteen, including one or two professors. I particularly enjoyed inviting students who were misfits—those who were usually not asked to go anywhere.

One day I was approached by a short-haired, knock-kneed girl named Betty Jane Smith, who was at least fifty pounds overweight and had never had a date. Normally she had a cheerful personality, but her head was lowered as she approached. "I understand you carry a bunch of kids to the Fifth Quarter every Monday," she said, looking down at her feet.

"That's right," I answered.

She glanced up hesitantly. "Can I go?"

"You'll be my special date," I said with a smile. "All you can eat, my treat."

That night, I watched her down nine orders of prime rib, and afterward she looked like she'd died and gone to heaven. She became a regular on Monday nights, and it was a thrill to see her light up, laugh at my corny jokes, and begin to tell jokes of her own. Since her father had died while she was in high school, I eventually became a kind of surrogate parent to her, advising her on many important decisions, and sometimes lending her money. However, our close, trusting relationship would never have developed had she not been welcomed with open arms on that first night.

One Monday night, a country girl from Louisiana joined us. At the salad bar, she followed behind a professor who covered his plate with anchovies. Though she didn't know what they were, she did the same thing. Immediately after taking her first bite, she grabbed a glass of water and guzzled it. With a sour grimace, she exclaimed, "This is the saltiest bacon I've ever eaten!" We almost fell out of our chairs laughing.

After the meal, one of the waitresses asked me, "Can I wait on y'all next Monday night when you come in? Y'all are about the happiest people I've ever seen."

"That's because we're Christians," I said. "We go to

Southeastern Bible College, and come here because we can stuff ourselves cheaply, and have a great time of fellowship."

"Well, it's an honor waiting on you."

"We'll ask for you next Monday," I said with a wink.

Often during these meals, the students would ask me to talk about my past. "Before I became a Christian, I often sloshed around in bars all night, thinking I was on top of the world," I told them. "Saturday nights I'd drink till I nearly passed out. But my body paid for it on Sunday mornings when I woke up with train whistles blowing in my head. That way of life led me straight to jail. I didn't know what fun really was until I met Jesus."

"Don't you ever feel bitter?" one of the students asked. "After all, you lost nine-and-a-half years of your life."

"How can I be bitter? Look where I am now. I'm sitting here with fourteen Christians, having the time of my life. I've got to rejoice! In prison I dreamed about being with fellow Christians, and not having to worry about getting drunk. Man, this is heaven sitting here guzzling gallons of ice tea, laughing, enjoying life. It took prison to get me here."

Sometimes one of the kids would say, "I'm sorry, Mr. Morris, but I can't go out Monday night; got a big test Tuesday."

"You're right, studying is important," I'd respond. "You need to work hard and get good grades. But you also need to laugh and have some fun."

I think Christ understood how to enjoy life. He didn't stifle His tears, but neither did He cover up His laughter and joy. He was criticized by the stuffy-headed Pharisees for the amount of time He devoted to parties and fun and playing with swarms of kids. Some of His parables told of tremendous banquets and rollicking wedding feasts—great times of joy. "I think we need to take joy as seriously as He did," I told the group.

At Southeastern, surrounded by young adults, I learned that faith can be fun. Lying on my bed in prison, I didn't know what fun was. I'd go stir crazy, thinking there had to be something more to the Christian life than I was experiencing. The kids showed me that "something more." I saw in them a vibrant, active love for Christ. When I was their age, I had no dreams or goals other than to get drunk on the weekend. These kids wanted to be ministers and missionaries. They wanted to be teachers and doctors. I'd missed out on my growing up years because I associated with the wrong crowd. These kids didn't know it, but I wanted to be like them. Because I was older, they turned to me for advice and help with their problems; because they were younger, I turned to them for joy-filled companionship. It was a perfect match.

Despite all the good times, my schedule was often grueling. After a full week at school, I'd hop into the car and drive a hundred or two hundred miles or more to speak. Sometimes I drove all night after a Sunday evening church service to make class Monday morning. On longer drives, I'd stop at a rest stop and sleep in my car. When there wasn't a rest stop, I'd sleep by the side of the road. Before long, I started getting invitations to travel greater distances, and so I'd fly to a speaking engagement. At times, I only kept going because I believed I was doing what God had called me to do.

I never asked for money when I spoke, though most churches would at least try to cover my expenses. But I assured them I understood if they couldn't even do that. There were times when they couldn't, but other times when they just *wouldn't*. Sometimes the treatment I received from a church was downright deceitful. It was a rude shock to discover that a few Christians could cheat and lie. More than once, a love offering would bring in far more than the church leaders thought appropriate. They'd hand me one or two hundred dollars and pocket the rest. That was hard to understand and accept.

One time I was asked to speak at the mayor's prayer breakfast in a large northern city. "Listen, Harold, I've heard good things about you," the caller said. "If you come, we'll help you with school. We want to be a part of what you're doing."

I told the man I was already scheduled to speak in Americus, Georgia, the evening of the same day.

"No problem," he said. "We'll fly you in the night before. You'll speak at the breakfast here at eight o'clock, and we'll have you on a plane by eleven. You won't have any problem reaching your destination in time."

So, that's what I did. There must have been eight hundred people at the breakfast, and many trusted Christ. On the way to the airport, my host broke down. Through his tears, he said, "God has used you in my life, Harold. In fact, because of what you said today, I'm thinking about going into full-time service for God."

At the airport he said, "We haven't counted the money yet, but we'll send you an honorarium check and reimbursement for the plane ticket. We'll take care of you, guaranteed. You see, Harold, we want to be a part of what you're doing."

I thanked him again for inviting me, and then asked that he rush the money for the plane ticket. "I had to charge the ticket because I didn't have the money," I said. "So would you please at least do that?"

"Oh, we're going to take care of you," he assured me with a big smile.

I went on to Americus, Georgia, arriving just in time to speak. After a full Sunday schedule, I flew home first thing Monday morning for classes. I was worn out, but God had blessed. And I figured that the honorarium from the Mayor's Prayer Breakfast would help a great deal. They had budgeted a portion of the ticket price for that purpose.

Tuesday night, my host from the prayer breakfast called and said, "People are still talking, Harold! Do you think you could come back and speak in our schools?" I told him I would consider the offer, but that my college schedule wouldn't permit it in the immediate future. "You've touched my life in a tremendous way," he said, "and I just know the schools here would welcome you with open arms. As for the breakfast, you'll be getting your money real soon. Real soon."

That was 1979. I never did receive the money or hear back from that man, and I had to borrow money to pay for the expenses incurred. That was a rude awakening for me. The Bible told me God owns the cattle on a thousand hills. The trouble was that some of God's people had fenced off their corner of the range, and wouldn't share the beef. I learned the hard way that faith must be content, as Paul says, with plenty or with poverty. My contentment necessarily came with the latter, but God used people's inconsideration to test the toughness of my faith.

In Matthew 25:23 the Bible says that if you've been faithful over a few things, you will be put in charge over many things. I determined that whatever resources God entrusted to me, I would always be willing to share with those who were in need.

One day the dean of students at Southeastern Bible College told me that one of the students, a girl named Sasha from Nigeria, would have to leave school. She was living with a family, but they'd told her they could no longer take care of her, and asked her to move out immediately.

"I don't know what I'm going to do," he said. "She has no money, no place to go."

"I don't understand," I countered. "You have vacant dorm rooms right here on campus, don't you?"

"Yes."

"Then why would she have to leave? Just put her in one of the dorms."

"You don't understand. We don't have any money for situations like this."

It didn't seem right that a girl who had sacrificed to come to Bible school in this country and had then fallen on hard times should be turned out on the streets. So I marched over to the registrar and said, "You give Sasha one of the empty dormitory rooms. You feed her and educate her. Then send me the bill. But don't kick her out." I asked that the girl never be told who paid her fees.

That experience caused me to think about my motivations for giving. Before I was a Christian, I was considered generous, but for very different reasons. My motivations were selfish. The bottom line was, "What's in it for me?" I didn't mind helping someone if I knew I could get something out of the deal, or if I knew he could do something for me later. There were always strings attached. That was the major way I gained and used influence in prison.

Then I met Christ and my attitude changed. I learned how to be content. Perhaps it helped that in prison, my life didn't center around material things. Everyone had three sets of prison clothes. We all ate the same meals. All I wanted was an occasional Pepsi and a few sweets. Realizing the extent of God's free gift to me, I cut the strings attached to my giving. I began to realize that my possessions weren't really mine; everything I had belonged to God. Anything I didn't need could be used to help other people.

That semester, Sasha went all over the school trying to learn who paid her bill. She was obsessed with finding out, but no one knew, and the registrar wouldn't tell her. After our final exams, I found an envelope marked "Harold" inside my mailbox. I opened it to find a note from Sasha, thanking me for providing for her. She went on to say she'd made the Dean's List, and would return home to her family in Nigeria after graduation. She explained that she had nine brothers and sisters, and that her dream was to witness to them and see them become Christians. "I just want to thank you, because God used you in a mighty way in my life," she closed.

Though I was grateful for the note, I was mad because I hadn't wanted her to know I'd paid the bill.

Later that day as I was sitting in the Student Union Building, Sasha walked over and sat down near me without saying anything. I looked over at her and said, "Sasha, I just want you to know that your note meant a great deal to me. I thank God I was able to help you this semester. I'm very proud of you."

She looked at me, started crying, and then threw her arms around me. "So you were the one that paid the bill!" she said.

"Of course," I responded. "You already knew that. I have your note right here."

"You don't understand," she said. "I didn't write the note to you, because I didn't know who paid the bill. I wrote the note to the anonymous person, and the registrar must have written your name on the envelope."

Though I had inadvertently given myself away, I felt great because God had again enabled me to help somebody else. I hadn't counted my money and said, "Well, I've got twenty dollars, and maybe I can give ten." I gave unconditionally, because I realized Jesus gave unconditionally to me.

There were many times when I gave away my last twenty dollars, but nobody knew that. Some professors said, "Old Harold, he must be loaded." Everybody thought I was rich. They didn't realize that over and over again God used other people to provide for me. I'd speak somewhere, and somebody would come up and hand me a wad of bills. Or I'd get a check in the mail from someone who'd write, saying, "I've got some extra money and feel led to give you three hundred dollars."

What hurt were the times I was misunderstood. There were those who thought I didn't deserve the opportunities God provided for me. They thought that because I was an ex-con, I was second-rate. In their minds, they deserved what was coming my way.

One Friday I was wearing a suit, all set for a quick getaway after class. One of my friends said, "Hey you in the suit! Where are you speaking this weekend?"

"West Palm Beach, Florida!" I said. "I'm speaking at the mayor's prayer breakfast in the morning and would appreciate your prayers." The large crowd that would be there didn't excite me; I was just thrilled I could speak for Jesus.

Another student, Stan Jackson, was listening to our conversation. He was a tall, handsome senior with excellent grades. I'd heard him speak in chapel before the entire student body, and he was a great orator, with extensive knowledge of Scripture. It seemed obvious that God would use him in a tremendous way. He had all the credentials, all the ability.

After hearing about my trip, Stan looked at me for a long moment, then leaned over and said, "Why you?"

I gave him a puzzled look. "I beg your pardon?"

"I mean, why do you get all these opportunities to speak? Why not other students? I don't understand why everything is given to you."

Several other students were listening by now. I glared at the young man and replied, "What you're really saying is, why not *you*?"

He shrugged. "Not necessarily, although I *am* graduating with straight A's. And I know how to preach, but the doors are not open for me like they are for you."

"That's exactly right, and they never will open with that attitude," I said. "You see, you're no good to God. You've got a good brain, but your heart's shot. You think I don't know the Scriptures as well as you, and you're probably right. Beyond that, you think I'm just an ex-con who's been taken in by this school, and who really shouldn't be studying the Word of God.

"You've got ability I don't have," I continued. "But the best abilities are *availability* and *dependability*, and you have neither. Buddy, you need a heart transplant. Instead of saying, 'Why you?' you should be praying for me right now that God will use me in the morning, that lost souls will turn to Christ, and that I'll have a safe trip. You should be excited that God's given me this opportunity."

A few days later, Stan apologized. We eventually became good friends, and he began to pray for me regularly. But it took that confrontation for him to realize God can do more with someone who is eager, willing, and available than someone who has all the qualifications, but is standing by the roadside criticizing others.

Beyond finances, there remained some difficult lessons for me to learn at school, particularly when it came to accepting authority. I was by no means the model student. When I didn't agree with a certain rule or an official decision, I challenged it. Usually I wasn't very graceful. The old con in me forced a confrontation, and sometimes those confrontations were ugly.

One of the most difficult periods for me was when I learned that the school had placed certain restrictions on my admittance. Because of my divorce many years earlier, I couldn't participate in the pastor's program. I learned that after I tried to sign up for a homiletics class and was informed I couldn't enroll.

Furious, I barged into the office of James Raiford, the dean of faculty. "Why didn't you just tell me I couldn't take your classes before I came to this school?" I asked. "I don't know what I'm doing here. Obviously, you think I'm a second-rate Christian and don't belong in the ministry."

Dean Raiford let me spout off, but said he did not have the authority to overrule school policy. That weekend I talked with my pastor back in South Carolina. "I'm quitting," I told him. "I'm tired of being a second-class Christian. Why do they keep throwing my past back at me? Why is it okay to be an ex-con, but because I made a mistake long before I was a Christian, I can't minister now. I tell you, I've had it. I'm quitting."

"Go ahead and quit," Pastor Norris countered, obviously upset by my attitude. "You're pretty good at it. You quit your first marriage, you quit your first college, you quit your first jobs. So why not quit Bible school, too."

"But they're wrong," I argued. "They have no right to do this."

"Maybe they are wrong. But so what? Are you going to let the fact that they won't let you take a few courses keep you from serving the Lord? You aren't planning to be a pastor anyway, so don't let this ruin you. You need the degree. You quit and your testimony will be destroyed."

Those words were a well-timed slap in the face that I needed. Pastor Norris was right. It was important that I have a piece of paper indicating I'd graduated. I needed some credibility in the eyes of the world. I was a loser. I'd been in prison. I needed to finish something, to separate myself from others, to become a Bible college graduate. It would help give legitimacy to my work. The following Monday I was back in school.

Gradually, I realized how much the professors and administrators at the college loved me. Sure, they made mistakes like everybody else. Dean Raiford admitted during one of our many discussions, "We don't know everything. We've all got feet of clay. We're going to fail. But we learn from those failures and move on." I realized it took tough faith to admit our weaknesses.

As the time of my graduation approached, Dean Raiford and I met often at a little coffee shop near the school. There we discussed my studies and talked about my life and future ministry. One day I told him I was thinking about continuing my education and eventually earning a Ph.D.

"Why would you want to do something like that?" he asked with a hearty laugh.

"Because it would help my testimony. It would help me win people to Christ. I'd be *Doctor* Harold Morris."

"Degrees and titles can't lead one person to Christ. You should be more concerned about your testimony for Jesus than earning a fancy name for yourself."

"What do you mean?"

"Think for a minute about some of the most influential people in the Bible. Who had more influence: Daniel, a humble servant in the King's court, or Nebuchadnezzar, King of Babylon, the most powerful nation on earth at that time? How about Moses or Pharaoh? Elijah or Queen Jezebel? Jesus or Pilate? Pharaoh, Jezebel, and Pilate all had the titles and honors. But Moses, Elijah, and, of course, our Lord Jesus Christ, had far more influence. The important thing to remember is that we must be faithful to the task God has given us. Then His work will prosper and His name will be glorified."

"You're right," I said.

"Concentrate on your testimony, Harold. But at the same time, realize that maintaining a strong testimony is no easy task. When you're faithful to Jesus Christ, it will cost you something. You'll often be misunderstood, even by your closest friends and family members. You will face constant attacks from an enemy you can't even see. Faithfulness to Christ may cost you your home, your ambition, your life. Often you won't even see the results of your labors. Your full reward will not come until after your work is completed. But serving Christ is a great challenge. Never forget that, Harold. It's costly and challenging, but no other life offers greater rewards."

"Sir, I want to accept that challenge," I said soberly, wondering what it would cost me to follow Christ.

My final term I took twenty-three hours, enabling me to graduate in three years instead of four. The heavy load meant a drop in my grades from *A's* and *B's* to *B's* and *C's*. But I graduated on May 16, 1981. The day before the ceremony, I received the incredible news that the Governor of Georgia had issued me a pardon. My crime was done away with, and my rights as a citizen of the United States were restored. I was now truly free. As a

Bible school graduate I could go anywhere and minister as God's servant.

During the graduation ceremony, as I walked across the stage to receive my diploma my eyes met those of Dean Raiford. "I'm proud of you, Harold," he said. "I'm proud to call you my friend and God's servant."

For me, being God's servant meant there was a whole world full of needs I could help meet. It meant innumerable opportunities to minister and to exercise tough faith. Where would I begin? I didn't know. But before doing anything, I needed some time to learn God's direction.

Chapter Seven

A BETTER WAY

For the first time in nearly fifteen years, I was truly free. The long duration spent behind bars and then reporting to parole officers was over. Graduation from Bible school ended the rigors of classes, homework, and tests. Now I could make my own decisions about where to live, what to buy, and where to travel.

All I had to my name was a car, a few clothes, a trunk full of books, and confusion about my future. I needed time to sort out my emotions, to think, to pray, and learn exactly what God wanted me to do. Clebe McClary, my one-armed spiritual father, provided me with a place to do that. He and his wife were going away for the summer, and they invited me to live in their South Carolina beach home. All I had to do was pay the utilities and phone bill.

One event I had to resolve in my mind was Becky's marriage. She had called a few months earlier. Her voice was bubbly, and it was obvious she'd won the long, hard battle with grief.

"I've met the most wonderful man!" she had announced. "His name is Max Greer. I wanted you to be the first to know!" She related how their pastors and wives had arranged their dinner date meeting, and how much she and Max had in common. He was a widower with two children and a deep love for the Lord. "I believe he's God's man for me. He's right," she said.

I tried to rejoice with her, but it was difficult. Even though I had told her I wasn't husband material and had sincerely prayed God would bring a godly man into her life, I had to admit Becky and her daughter were an important part of my life. Now another man was replacing me; I was no longer needed.

"He sounds too good to be true. He's probably a con artist," I said, only half joking. "You'll see. He's probably a fly-by-nighter. Just wait until you get to know him a little better."

Fortunately, Becky didn't take my words seriously. Maybe she was sensitive enough to realize I couldn't express to her the mixture of happiness and pain I felt. Her big day was shortly after my graduation, and though she'd sent me a wedding invitation, I decided to stay at the beach the day she became Becky Smith-Greer. It seemed better to slip quietly out of her life. Meanwhile, I prayed for her and Max, that their marriage would be long and happy.

That summer of 1981 was a lonely time. Many days were spent walking on the beach, thinking, and praying. I was forty-three, an age when most men my age were settled into good jobs and nice homes. They were married and had kids in high school and even college. I was twenty years behind and struggling to maintain proper perspective. I forced myself to hold firm to my conviction, reinforced repeatedly by Dean Raiford, that true security was not found by accumulating things, money, or degrees. True security was my relationship with Jesus Christ. I also had to force myself to hold firm in my heart what I knew in my head: faith must be patient. God had taken care of me so far; certainly He wouldn't let me down now.

Each morning I'd wake before dawn and watch the sun rise over the ocean. I'd walk on the sand long before anyone was on the beach, or sit and listen to the calming sound of the waves while praying for God to reveal His will for my life. I'd open my Bible and read, often meditating on the words from Isaiah 40:30-31: "Even youths grow tired and weary, and young men stumble and fall; but those who hope in the Lord will renew their strength. They will soar on wings like eagles; they will run and not grow weary, they will walk and not be faint." That's what I needed—renewed strength. That, and some direction.

To determine God's will for my life, I thought back to the day I was released from Georgia State Penitentiary. Early that morning, just three hours before the guard unlocked my cell for the last time, I got on my knees and thanked God for my life and freedom. At that time, I was reminded of the final words of Jesus before He ascended into Heaven: ". . . You will be my witnesses in Jerusalem, and in all Judea and Samaria, and to the ends of the earth" (Acts 1:8). On my knees, I had made a commitment. For the rest of my life I would make young people my Jerusalem, prisoners my Judea, and churches my Samaria. I told God I would go anywhere to serve Him.

Gradually the picture unfolded as I thought of the Great Commission of Jesus, to "go and make disciples of all nations, baptizing them in the name of the Father and of the Son and of the Holy Spirit, and teaching them to obey everything I have commanded you" (Matt. 28:19-20). In light of those instructions, I wrote down the following goals:

1] To be a positive role model to kids in schools throughout America, to reach them for Jesus, and to disciple them;

2] To visit prisons and reproduce myself by winning inmates to the Lord, teaching them the ways of God, and educating them; and

3] To visit churches, challenging young people and their parents to build their lives and families on the foundation of Christ, become active members, and draw others into the church.

"Lord," I prayed, "I will speak every day You open the doors, I will go anywhere I'm invited, and I will never ask for money. You will have to provide for my needs."

My vision was clarified, yet one question persisted: How would I start? I had no organization. I had no money. What was the first step? Then one day, sitting on the sand, the thought struck me, *Dummy, who have you always gone to for advice? Who encouraged you to go to Bible college? Who supported you all the way? Who has always been there in your life no matter what?* There were two men, Bobby Richardson and Bob Norris. It was time to go to them for counsel. I visited Bobby first.

"I've been waiting for you to come," he said, handing me a list of men who wanted to be part of my ministry. "Pray about each of them, Harold. They love you. And they, too, are waiting for you. They'll help you get organized and provide you with both financial advice and spiritual wisdom.

Then I visited my pastor, Bob Norris, and three other men whom Bobby had recommended. They agreed to become the board of directors for Harold Morris Ministries and provide the support group I needed. However, they didn't want to make things easy for me.

With their counsel, my first act was to sell my Chevy for $3,000 and lease another auto. After the initial car payments, there remained $2,500 to launch my work. Starting in September, I would drive through the Southeast and speak in schools, prisons, and churches.

Shortly before I hit the road for my first extended tour, I had a visit from Malcolm, the filthy teenager I'd rescued from the county jail and taken for a visit to Georgia State Penitentiary while I was working at the boys' home. I hardly recognized him now that he was wearing a golf shirt and slacks instead of a T-shirt and tattered jeans. He greeted me with a hug and told me how much I meant to him. "Mr. Morris, I'll never forget Big Mac and that kiss!" he said. "Because of that day, my life changed. I'm in college now and engaged to a wonderful girl. And I'm thinking about going into the ministry."

What an encouragement to see the evidence of tough faith reproduced. It reinforced again that God had called me to work with young people. My background, coupled with God's grace, gave me a unique blend of love, humor, understanding, and tenacious strength to challenge and help them.

As I traveled around speaking, there were times I needed all of those qualities. At a high school in South Carolina, I was five minutes into my speech when a boy in the front row started laughing and cutting up with his cronies.

"Hold it!" I said. "You there in the front row, shut your mouth. Me or you, one's got to go."

"I don't believe nothin' you've said," the well-built kid shouted back.

Suddenly smiles appeared on the faces of students and teachers everywhere. This kid was obviously the school bully, and everyone was eager to see who would win this confrontation. "You don't believe anything I've said today?" I asked. "What you're really saying is that you use drugs."

"I didn't say that!" he protested.

"Hey punk, you wouldn't have interrupted me if you weren't a drug user, because I'm talking about drugs. I say you're a coward if you don't stand up and tell this student body you're a drug user."

The kid rose slowly. "Yeah, I've used drugs," he announced.

"That's right. And how did I know? 'Cause you're a punk, just like I used to be. That's the reason you're running your mouth. And let me tell you something, boy. You'd better be good to me, 'cause with the lifestyle you're living, one day you're going to wind up in prison, and the only friend you'll have in the world is me. I'm going to come see you on Sundays, bring you peanut butter and jelly sandwiches, and tell you I love you. Nobody else in the world will care. So be nice to me now, understand?"

The entire audience burst into applause. When they quieted down, I told the kid, "Now sit down and listen, because I want to tell you how to avoid prison. I'm going to tell you how to change your life."

When I finished my talk, I stepped off the stage, walked toward the boy, and stuck out my hand. He accepted my handshake, and then I put my arm around him and led him over to a corner to talk. After I learned that his name was Marcus, I asked him to tell me about his life. He said he had moved there from New York City to live with his grandmother, because nobody else cared about him. He was a street kid who found it hard adjusting to life in a small southern town.

I had agreed to spend the rest of the day visiting several classrooms. So I called the principal over and said, "If it's all right with you, I'd like Marcus to stay with me for the rest of the day." He had no objection. In each class, I introduced Marcus, saying, "This is my tight man. The warden assigned him to be my bodyguard." The boy stuck out his chest in pride.

At the end of the day, Marcus followed me to the parking lot.

"Mr. Morris," he began, "I just want you to know I'm going to try to change my life. I'll never forget this day."

"Son, I want to tell you something," I responded. "You can be anything in the world you want to be. Now that you know what to do, go do it. Remember, you're special. God made you just like you are. I know you're going through difficult times, but I can tell you're a leader. You just make sure you become the right kind of leader. No more drugs, alcohol, or illicit sex. I know you can stop. Promise me you will?" He promised, and as I drove away, I saw him in my rearview mirror, waving good-bye with one hand, wiping tears from his eyes with the other.

That was my work, to recognize young kids like me and channel them in the right direction. In a sense, my work with teens was a prison ministry—I was striving to keep them out of jail. I particularly related to them in the areas of negative peer pressure, alcohol, drugs, and sex because I'd ruined my life as a young man in those areas. I wanted to show them a better way. Toward that end, in each personal encounter I tried to determine where a person was spiritually and then help him take the next step toward Christian maturity.

Sometimes that meant shaking up misguided Christians. One morning I spoke at a large high school in Alabama. Before I went on stage, I talked to the student body president who would introduce me. He said he was a Christian, and when I asked about his spiritual condition he replied, "Everything is going great."

"Tell me something," I said. "Do other students know you're a Christian?"

"Yes, sir, I believe they do."

"Are you witnessing?"

"Yes, sir. You'd be proud of me, Mr. Morris."

"Tell me about it."

"Well you see, I don't witness with my lips. Mr. Morris, I want people to see Christ in me, and that way they won't feel like I'm forcing Jesus down their throats. I don't like to run around telling people about Him. I want my *life* to be the Gospel."

"I know you're sincere," I said. "But it happens that you're sincerely wrong."

"Mr. Morris?"

"I'm really disappointed in you," I continued as his jaw dropped lower. There was hurt in his eyes. "Son, nobody will ever experience eternal life based on your life. People are saved by Jesus' *death*. Your life must reflect Jesus, but how will they know about His death and resurrection unless your mouth tells them?"

A few minutes later when the young man introduced me, he apologized to the entire student body. He admitted that he'd lived a quiet, easy Christian faith. Then he said, "I'd like to introduce you to a man who knows that faith is neither."

My travels taught me a lot about faith. During my first twelve months on the road, I spoke more than four hundred times. There were days when I spoke seven times—to six high school groups, plus a rally at night. Not all of the talks were to large assemblies. I'd talk to football teams, Bible studies, a handful of troubled kids, basically any gathering that would have me.

According to my promise to God, I never charged for my speaking. Sometimes I was paid an honorarium, but it didn't always cover my travel expenses. Once I spent two weeks holding meetings in one southern community. By the time I finished paying for my motel, food, and gas, I was several hundred dollars in the hole. The thought crossed my mind that if things didn't pick up, working for the Lord would bankrupt me. But I didn't quit. I just prayed harder that God would see me through the lean times, while continuing to use my life to win others to Christ.

Inevitably, someone felt led to help financially when I needed it the most. However, it was very tempting to entertain the job offers that came my way. Businessmen told me, "Harold, you're a born salesman. You could make a fortune." I was offered well-paying jobs selling everything from seafood and lumber, to insurance and detergent. At night, alone in a motel room, a little voice in my mind would say, "Hey Harold, why don't you leave this rat race? Take that job and make something of your life."

"But I can't," my conscience argued. "I'm doing what God told me to do."

"Harold, you're broke," the first voice would counter. "You've never had anything. What's so wrong with going out and earning a little money. You deserve to have a nice car and a home of your own. Find yourself a wife, settle down, and have some kids."

Again my conscience kicked in: "Why do I say I have nothing? I've always had food and shelter. God has always provided everything I've needed. I have a car, and I'm able to pay the rent on my apartment. What more do I need?"

"But just think, if you spent all the hours selling that you spend ministering for nothing, you'd be a millionaire."

"No! I won't turn my back on God. I owe everything to Him. I begged Him for my freedom, and He brought me out of prison. He's given me everything I asked for. I can't reject His call now. It's not right, and He won't bless it."

Each time as the confrontation ended, I knew that my faith had grown another notch. This was where tough faith was most needed—not in the high-profile, dramatic moments before hundreds of students in a school assembly, but in the private moments when Satan dangled before me the riches of the world and bid me to follow him.

Those solitary battles strengthened me for the challenge that faced me in the schools. Every invitation was an opportunity to help build the faith of young people, to help them recognize the barriers and break through them. But I could only lead them as far as I allowed God to take me in my faith.

My favorite invitation was one that allowed me to spend an entire day at one school. Then I could do so much more than address a large assembly. I could have some significant interaction with individuals and small groups. One of my most memorable days was at a high school in Alabama.

I met the principal, Mr. Hampton, in his office half an hour before the assembly was scheduled to begin. After asking him how much time I had, I said, "Sir, I'm a Christian, and I like to talk about what Jesus Christ has done in my life. I would like to include that in my talk to the kids. However, I understand that might cause you problems, and I don't want to abuse the opportunity you've given me. Is it all right to mention the name of Jesus?"

"No, Harold, I'd probably have a call from some disgruntled parent if you did." His response was typical of most school administrators.

"Then I'll tell you what. I won't mention the name of Jesus if you won't."

"You got a deal."

As I followed Mr. Hampton to the gym, he explained that this was the first assembly the school had held in some time. "We don't hold very many because the kids just won't listen. I'd better warn you it will be noisy."

"Thank you for the warning, sir, but I'm not worried. I believe I can hold their attention." There were five black girls standing in a group as we talked. I pointed over to them and said, "I'll show you what I mean. See those five girls. If you'll stand here, I guarantee I can walk over and make them scream."

"This I've got to see."

So I strutted over to them, put my arms around two of the girls and leaned into their huddle. "You bad!" I said to them with a grin. "You big bad mamma jamma. You bad as you can be!"

Sure enough, the girls screamed with glee. "You our speaker?" asked one. When I told her I was, she said, "You're pretty cool for a white dude."

After the principal introduced me to the packed gymnasium, I asked the kids to indicate if they thought I really looked like a convict. "Suppose I had on a three piece suit like your principal. If you didn't know I was a convict, which one of us would you think had spent ten years in prison. Me?"

The kids yelled "NO!"

"How about Mr. Hampton?"

"YES!" they shouted, laughing and clapping as the principal winced.

"Young people, I've done you a big favor today. I've gotten you out of class for an hour. Now all I ask is that you return the favor; that you listen to me. You see, not that many years ago, I was sitting where you are. I had all the potential you have, but I blew it. I was an all-state athlete in high school. I was captain of the football, basketball, and baseball teams. I had numerous scholarship offers. But I said, "I'm not going to college. I'm going to drink beer, chase girls—that's the life.' So that's what I did for a period of time.

"Finally my dad told me I had to go to work. I got a job. I got married. I enrolled in college. Everything was going great. But my senior year, I dropped out of school, divorced my wife, and said, now I'm free to do as I please. I began to go to night-clubs, and there I met prostitutes, drug addicts, and ex-convicts. Young people, it took one year to destroy my life."

I told my story, about meeting two men at a nightclub and going with them to Atlanta to party for a week. I explained how, as we were leaving Atlanta, my friends held up a grocery store, and in the process shot an innocent bystander. One year later, I said, the FBI arrested me, my two friends testified against me, and I was given two life sentences for robbery and murder. "Young people, don't feel sorry for me. I got what I deserved. I consorted with the scum of the earth, and I became what they were. I tell you today, the people you associate with will deter-mine the outcome of your life, good or bad."

My talk was a mixture of my life story and warnings to the young people, who listened intently to every word I spoke. I discussed negative peer pressure, drugs, alcohol, illicit sex, and teenage suicide. I illustrated every point with stories from my years in prison to show how the decisions they made at young ages could directly affect the rest of their lives.

When I finished my message, I announced that any teacher who wanted me to visit his class that day could sign up at the office. And then I fielded questions. "Feel free to ask anything," I said. "You can even ask me why I'm so handsome."

Everyone laughed, and several hands went up, including Mr. Hampton's. I immediately acknowledged him.

"Mr. Morris, would you please tell us how you got out of prison?" the principal asked.

"Sir, on February 18, 1974, a man came to visit me in prison. He told me he loved me and gave me a Bible. I read that Bible, gave my heart to the Lord, and He freed me."

A group of hands started waving for my attention. I recognized a boy who asked, "Is it difficult living a Christian life behind prison bars?"

I turned to the principal. "May I answer that?" He indicated I could, so I proceeded to tell the students about how I grew spiritually in prison. So while the principal originally had limited my message, during the question and answer session I was able to present the Gospel in a manner that offended no one.

I called on one little girl who asked, "Mr. Morris, why are your two little fingers so crooked?"

"You like those?" I asked. I held up my hands to show that my pinkies were indeed permanently bent at forty-five degree angles. "These fingers are so handy. They're great for picking lint out of my naval. Or how about cleaning ears?" I stuck my little fingers in my ears and rotated them a couple of times for the howling crowd. "You want to know how I got these?" I continued. "My right one was bent in a fight during a prison basketball game. The left one was broken when I fell on it, and the prison hospital didn't set it right. So I got a matched set."

After the assembly, on the way to my first classroom, a girl handed me a pack of cigarettes. "I'm through smoking," she said.

"That's good, honey," I said. "I'm glad you won't be spoiling your pretty face anymore with those cigarettes."

Then she handed me her matches. "Take these, too. I'm serious."

"I'm proud of you. You're taking a stand. Jesus can't make a decision for you. You have to do that. But when you make that decision, He will give you the strength, power, and courage to overcome your smoking or any other problem you have."

I enjoyed talking with kids in a classroom far more than an assembly. In the gym, many of the kids were embarrassed to ask a question, but in the class they were among friends and felt more freedom to talk about the issues that affected their lives. "I don't have all the answers," I said after the teacher introduced me and told the kids they could ask me anything they wanted. "I've come here today because I love you, and if you have a problem, you write me or call me collect. We'll work it out together." I passed out a stack of cards with my name, address, and phone number.

In the first class, a group of giggling girls sat together on one side of the room. "Will you look at these angels? They must have had recess in heaven," I quipped. And then turning my attention to the girls, I pointed at several boys and said, "Now you stay away from these sorry rascals, hear?"

That naturally sparked a discussion about dating. "You know, you girls probably think beauty is everything. Let me tell you something. When I was in high school, I was the meanest student there. One day I told this girl, 'You's ugly.' Well, she looked at me and said, 'Beauty is only skin deep.' And I said, 'Honey, with you ugly goes all the way to the bone.' "

When the laughter died down I finished the story. "I just saw that same girl not long ago. You know what she said? 'You were right. Ugly does go all the way to the bone. I'm looking at you!' But let me tell you. She's married, has two kids, and today she's *beautiful*. You know why? She always had a beautiful personality. She had character. She cared about her appearance. She went to college and got an education. Because of that, she's become a beautiful woman, and has let Jesus Christ direct her life."

One of the girls tried to ask a question about sex. "It's like the guys have only one thing on their mind. And sometimes I wish we could just have a good time without getting, you know, physical and all."

"Honey, the problem with most teenagers is that they wait till they're in the backseat of an automobile to make a decision," I said. "You'll fail every time if you do that. Girls, let me tell you what to look out for when you're on a date. The sorry rascal takes you out, and he parks. He thinks he's a cool dude in the groove. He looks over at you and says, 'Baby, you know what you are?' And you say, 'What?' He says, 'You are a T.F.' You ask, 'What in the world is a T.F.?' He says, 'You're a total fox.' And you start thinking this guy is pretty nice. Then he looks at you and says, 'And it ain't gonna be long before you're a U.B.M.' Naturally you ask, 'What in the world is a U.B.M.?' He answers,

'An Ultra Bad Mamma.' Now you're thinking this guy is King Cool.

"But look out! The sorry rascal is setting you up. He'll look at you and say, 'If you love me, prove your love.' Listen to me. Anyone who asks you to prove your love doesn't love you. I used that same line years ago. He's not asking you to prove your love. He's asking you to commit immoral acts. He's asking you to surrender your virtue, throw away your self-respect, jeopardize your precious reputation, and risk getting pregnant or catching some disease. That's not love. Anyone who loves you wants what's *best* for you."

One of the girls meekly asked, "But, what are we to do? Some guys can be so persistent."

"Let me tell you how you deal with that character. Take your Bible with you on the date. Put it on the seat between you. By the time he crawls over Matthew, Mark, Luke, and John, he'll be worn out. He might not ask you out again, but he's doing you a favor.

"I know what you girls want," I continued. "You want a macho man. And all you guys want a macha girl. But that's not what you need. You need a *natcho* man and a *natcha* girl. That's the person who stands up and says to Satan, 'I'm natcho man' and 'I'm natcha girl!' "

After class was dismissed, one of the girls who'd sat quietly in a far corner came up to me. She started to cry as she said, "I wish I could have heard this two months ago. I really needed it then."

"Well, it's better late than never," I said. I looked at her and asked the question to which I already knew the answer. "Are you pregnant?"

She nodded.

"Have you told anyone?"

"No. My parents would kill me if they found out."

"What's your name?"

"Cynthia."

"Cynthia, there was a time when I thought it was too late for me. But it wasn't. It's never too late."

"I'd just like to get rid of this problem, to have it over with. No one would know."

"Honey, it's not a 'problem.' It's a baby; a human life. I know this is a terribly lonely time, and I'm sure it's tempting to think about an abortion. But I hope you'll think not just about your life, but also about the life of the baby inside you. Do you have a Bible at home?"

"Yes."

"Please do me a favor. Tonight would you read Psalm 139? Do that, and then prayerfully ask God what you should do. And then I want you to call me collect when we have more time to talk. Cynthia, I want to help you. Just promise you'll call."

"Okay."

"It's not too late. Together we can work this out. Every day is a new day when we love the Lord. He cares about you, and I care about you. You promise to call?"

"I promise."

After the next class, several student leaders escorted me to lunch. As I got in the cafeteria line, I saw the student body president, two cheerleaders, and several of the top athletes jock-eying for position near me. They didn't know I had other plans. This was my favorite time of the day. I knew there were some kids I needed to talk to, who would never have the courage to approach me. My eyes scanned the room and I quickly located the perfect table. Sitting there were two very lonely looking girls. Beside them was an even sorrier looking pimple-faced boy. They were all looking at me, unaware that I struggled with the same inferiority complex they did.

As I walked over and sat down across from the pimple-faced boy, I said, "Yo bro, you bad!" Even the boy started laughing. To the two girls, I said, "Hey there, foxy mammas!" and gave each of them a kiss on the cheek. They squealed with delight, and we were off on a wonderful half hour of fun and talk.

As lunch period was about to end, I looked at the young boy across from me. "You know, you're special," I said for all to hear. His eyebrows raised. "We're just alike. People tell us we're nobodies. We're not as good as them. But they're wrong. Did you know that Jesus loves you? You're special! The President of the United States—his kids can only say 'My dad's president.' The Queen of England—her kids can only say 'My mother's queen.' But let me tell you something . . ." I paused to make eye contact with many of the kids crowded around the table. "If you know Christ, you're royalty. Your Father's King of the universe! He made you just like you are. He loves you, and Harold Morris loves you, too."

After lunch I visited several more classrooms. When school was finally dismissed, a huge black kid built like Hercules came up to me. One of the students had already told me he was the school's outstanding athlete and was going to a major college on a football scholarship. "Mr. Morris, you're a great man," he said. "I've never had a father, and I was wondering if you would be my daddy."

Putting my arm around him, I said, "Son, I'm honored you'd want me to be your daddy. However, I'm afraid I wouldn't do a very good job, because I live in Atlanta, and am on the road all the time. But I'll always be available to help. You can come visit me, call me collect, write me. I'll help you any way I can." I then gave him my card, and he gave me a big hug.

That special day in Alabama was typical of the days I spent in schools. It was an exhilarating time of speaking, encouraging, and counseling. My reward was not financial, but seeing the response of so many young people who were hungry for love. It was also frustrating that there wasn't more time to spend individually with them. That is why I encouraged them to write and call. And many of them did. One girl wrote and told me she had kept my card on her mirror for two years before contacting me.

Cynthia was one of the girls with whom I followed up. We had several phone conversations over the next few months. One day I received a letter from her saying she'd followed my advice not to have an abortion. "I want to thank you for loving me and caring. You were so right. That boy who got me pregnant has never spoken to me to this day. In fact, he laughs at me when he sees me.

"I dropped out of school for a term to have the baby and now that I'm back, I've been able to help other girls with similar problems," she continued. "That makes it all worthwhile. I've got the most beautiful baby on earth. Even though I've scarred my life and that of my child, I'm so thankful I listened to you."

Sometimes the principal tipped me off to someone with a problem. At a high school in Georgia, I was told about a sixteen-year-old girl who wanted to commit suicide. The principal called her up to the counselor's office where I met with her for an hour. "Honey, you're a beautiful girl," I said to her. "Why do you want to take your life?"

"I hate my parents," she answered. "They love my sister and hate me. I'm doing drugs, dating a man who's twenty, and having sex." She shook her head and said, "I know it's wrong, but I don't care. Life isn't worth living."

"I want you to know something. I love you very much. Would you do one favor for me? Would you call this number collect when you get ready to take your life? If you do, I promise I won't try to talk you out of suicide. I just want to choose the color of the casket, and blue's my favorite color."

She started giggling at my ridiculous humor. "I can call you collect?"

"Anytime."

Ten days later, on a Friday afternoon in mid-May, she called. "Mr. Morris, I'm getting ready to take my life."

"Where are you?"

She told me she was sitting in front of a National Guard Armory in a town about sixty miles north of Atlanta.

"I'm leaving right now. Please give me one hour." I hopped in my car and drove as fast as I could to the town. I had no idea where the Armory was, but somehow I managed to find it quickly. She was sitting on the curb, waiting. She got in the car, and we drove over to McDonald's.

For a while I told her some jokes and made her laugh. Finally I said, "Honey, what's the problem?"

"I tried to work things out with my Mom, but it's not happening. Yesterday I saw that man again, and he gave me drugs. I feel so guilty."

We talked for nearly three hours about her problems and how tough faith in Jesus Christ could change her life. Finally, I drove her home, and as we parked in her driveway, I said, "I'd like to ask another favor." I pulled some money out of my pocket and handed it to her. "Will you go and buy something nice for yourself? Then buy a gift for your mother. Sunday is Mother's Day. I want you to give your Mom that present and tell her you love her.

"I know you think your mom has failed you. But I'm sure she really does love you. Maybe she just doesn't know how to communicate her love. So you tell her you love her and that you've failed her. Say, 'Mom, I want to get to know you and love you.' If you will work at it, the two of you will learn to communicate."

The girl looked at me, and then reached over and kissed me on the cheek. With her hand on the door just before jumping out of the car, she asked, "Mr. Morris, who are you? I can't talk to my principal, my teachers, my parents. But you've been in prison a long time, and I told you things today that I've never told anyone. Who *are* you?"

There was really only one way to answer her. "Honey," I said, "I'm just a big old ugly trophy of God's grace."

That girl did not take her life. She gave up drugs and the twenty-year-old man, and things gradually improved with her parents. While I rejoiced at the reports in her letters and phone calls, I certainly couldn't take credit. It was simply another trophy of God's grace.

While much of my time was spent in schools, an equally important part of my ministry was visiting prisons. In particular, I looked for a few key inmates to disciple. That was God's plan, to make disciples, and I knew from experience how difficult the process was inside a prison. I also knew God could transform any life in any situation.

Chapter Eight

THE MIRACLE OF BAM BAM

Two preachers accompanied me on a trip into an Alabama prison in 1981. We were visiting from cell to cell when we approached a towering black man.

"My name's Harold Morris and these two guys are my preacher friends," I began. He looked at me and grunted. I started telling him that I was an ex-con who'd been saved in prison, when all of a sudden he spit in my face. I wiped my face with the back of my hand and glared at the inmate.

"You're not spitting on me, because I'm nobody," I said. "You're spitting on Jesus. He came to help people like you. But they spit on Him two thousand years ago, and they're spitting on Him now. I don't know who you are or what you're in prison for. But I do know that Jesus loves you despite—"

"I hate your guts," he interrupted, "and I hate the guts of your Jesus." Then he spit in my face again.

I was so upset I had tears in my eyes. "Let me tell you something," I said, taking a defiant step closer and pointing my crooked finger at him. "One day, you will get on your knees and trust Christ, or else you'll burn in the pit of hell."

He sneered at me and gave a short, sarcastic laugh.

"You see that commode?" I said, pointing to the toilet in his cell. "I took water out of a filthy commode in Georgia State

Penitentiary, and threw it in the face of the man who first tried to talk to me about Jesus. So I'm only getting what I deserve."

"Get out of my cell," he barked.

"I'll go, but you aren't done with me yet," I said. "I'm going out to my car to get you a Bible, and then I'm going to turn around and bring it right back to you."

When I went out to the car, one of the pastors insisted on taking the Bible back, because he was afraid the inmate would attack me. Though he was able to deliver the Bible without further incident, I didn't care. I was too upset. "This is it, I'm through," I spouted. "I'll never go in a prison again. No one's going to spit on me and humiliate me. I don't have to put up with it; I deserve better."

Later that night I calmed down and allowed God to speak to my heart. He reminded me once again that I didn't deserve better; that apart from Him I deserved death. Without realizing it, I had started thinking too highly of myself, believing I was above ridicule and humiliation. As the Lord popped my bubble, I felt Him saying, "I never asked you to be successful or esteemed. I never asked you to win converts, get a big head and start thinking you were the one responsible for results. I only asked you to be faithful. So what if a guy spits in your face because of Me? Don't worry about your image. Just concern yourself with being faithful and obedient."

Then He seemed to add, "I also want you to know that I'm proud of you for standing there and not running."

I learned a significant lesson that day: I can't save anyone. I'd often heard people say, "I led five to Christ," or, "I spoke in front of thousands, and 500 people came forward." It's tempting to think we save people. The truth is, Jesus saves them. My converts might last fifteen seconds; those of Jesus last forever. My responsibility was not to win converts, but to faithfully proclaim the Gospel.

With that realization, I got on my knees in my motel room and asked God to forgive me for having put my own reputation above His. After that I began visiting even more prisons. With each visit, I heard the still, small voice of approval from God: "Well done, my good and *faithful* servant."

The more prisons I visited, the more I was convinced that my prison ministry was not to be to the masses. Rather it would be based on intense discipling of a few inmates after they were won to Christ. I would identify those men who had hearts after God, educate them, and teach them to carry on their own ministry behind bars. That was the plan Jesus demonstrated when He took twelve men and poured His life into them. If it was good enough for Him, it was good enough for me.

I had to remember that just because an inmate became a Christian in prison did not mean God would automatically free him. In my case, I was released. But for every Harold Morris, there were dozens whom God was content to use while still incarcerated. Those men could be far more effective behind bars than me or anybody else coming in from the outside.

One of the prisons I visited regularly was the State Penitentiary in Columbia, South Carolina. In March 1982 I was asked to speak to the inmates there on death row. After I finished the warden told me about a problem he was having with one of the death row inmates. "Yesterday he almost killed a guard and another inmate. We've had to separate him from the population because he's a constant threat to everyone. Would you mind talking to him?"

"Not at all."

"Let me tell you about him. His name is Michael Godwin. He's only twenty, but he's the most dangerous criminal in the history of South Carolina. He's an animal. Everyone calls him Bam Bam because he's always hitting people. And he's fast. *Bam bam*, and it's all over."

"Why is he in prison?"

"He's been sentenced to die for the rape and murder of a young woman."

I was taken downstairs, beneath the main facility to a prison within a prison that reminded me of a medieval dungeon. Security was so tight that even guards were searched before entering the area. I was locked in a tiny, windowless room with a small desk and two chairs. As I waited, I tried to picture what kind of animal I would meet. I imagined a hulk of a man with scars all over his face. He would probably be missing an eye, and perhaps a finger or two.

When the door opened again, I saw a handcuffed young man, barely out of his teens, with a full head of red hair crowning a square face. He appeared to be about six-foot-one, with broad shoulders and two hundred and plenty pounds of solid muscle. The guard told me I had one hour. As he started to close the door, I asked if he'd remove the handcuffs from the young man.

"Oh no, he might hurt you." The guard slammed the door and left me looking into the eyes of Michael Godwin. Neither of us knew what to say.

"What do you want?" he finally demanded.

"The warden thought I might talk with you," I began tentatively. "I just got done speaking up on death row."

"Ain't none of this religion junk, is it?"

"Oh no, no! No religion, I promise." I swallowed hard and stepped forward to shake his hand. "I'm Harold Morris."

Michael squeezed my hand so hard that I was sure he was trying to break it.

"I'm sorry about the handcuffs," I said. "I wish I could take them off."

"Cut the small talk and tell me what you want."

"The warden tells me you're violent, that you almost killed a guard and an inmate yesterday."

"That's right."

"I don't believe you're violent."

"Step closer and say that!"

"I believe you're angry."

He gave me a quizzical look, and then asked me to repeat myself.

"I don't believe you're violent. I believe you're angry."

"That's it! I'm not violent; I'm just angry."

I breathed a sign of relief. "Thank You, Lord, thank You," I prayed silently. Then I looked him square in the eye and said,

"Tell me, who do you think I am? Do you think I'm a success in life?"

"Yeah, probably."

"What do you think I do?"

"Lawyer?"

"Nope."

"You got a tan. Golfer?"

I shook my head.

"Banker? Accountant? Teacher? Doctor? Reporter?"

"No on all counts."

"You're with the governor's office. You're a politician."

"No again."

"You could be anything."

"How long have you been locked up?"

"Six years."

"I've got you beat. I'm just like you, son. I was on death row in Georgia, sentenced to a double-life term for robbery and murder."

"You!"

"I did nearly ten years behind bars."

"Don't kid with me."

"I'm serious. Would you like to sit down? I'll tell you about it."

With the ice broken, we sat down and I told him about that fateful night in Atlanta when my two friends scrambled into my car and ordered, "Drive! Drive! We shot a man!" I explained how a year later the FBI arrested me, my friends testified against me, and the judge gave me two life sentences. And then I briefly told him how, after five years in prison, Christ changed my life, and outlined the details surrounding my parole and eventually pardon from the governor of Georgia.

When I was finished, I didn't wait for his reactions because I thought he might respond, despite his handcuffs, with a deft *bam bam*. So I quickly asked him to tell me his story.

I couldn't tell if he was shocked or surprised, but he apparently seemed pleased to have someone who truly wanted to listen to him. "Yesterday they stripped and shackled me spread-eagled to a steel spring mattress," he said. "The window was blown out, and they turned a fire hose on me full blast. I guess they were trying to punish me for hurting one of their friends. I beat a guard to a bloody pulp, and I probably would have killed somebody if they hadn't hosed me down."

"You've been in solitary since yesterday?"

"Yeah, got thrown in the dungeon last night. I was sick and tired of life, ready to give up. So I tore up my sheet, wove it into a real strong rope, and tied it to the top of the bars. I yanked on it to make sure it was solid, and then said a prayer. I said, 'Lord, I don't want to hurt anybody else, and I don't want anybody else to hurt me, either.' I stood up on my sink, tied the rope around my neck, and I prayed one more time, 'Lord, if I die, don't send me to hell.' When I jumped all the lights went out. I looked up, opened my eyes, and thought I had died. Then I saw the rope had broken! I couldn't believe it—I couldn't even kill myself! Then I loosened the noose so I wouldn't accidentally choke to death." He shook his head and smiled for the first time. "You talk about angry, I was angry. I wanted to kill somebody!"

I heard the guards coming down the hall, so I knew our time was almost over. As I stood up, Michael said, "Would you do me a favor?"

"I'll do anything for you, son."

"I don't want to trust Christ, like you said, but would you pray for me?"

"It would be an honor." I had a brief word of prayer for him before the guard opened the door. As I started to leave, I shook his hand, and again I felt he was trying to break it. "Michael, I've got to go, but I'll be back."

"Yeah, they all say that," he snorted.

Every Tuesday I made the five-hundred-mile round trip from Atlanta to Columbia to minister to inmates. But Michael was being punished and it was nearly two months before I saw him again. One day as the guards were shaking me down, I saw him. As soon as I passed through the door into death row, he ran up to me and said, "You came back!"

"I've been back every week," I told him.

"I know. I've checked."

Michael attended the service and stood beside me the whole time as I spoke to a small group of inmates. When we were finished, I gave Michael a Bible before parting.

The next week, when I spoke again, he was there holding his Bible. Afterward as I started to leave, I felt a nudge on my shoulder. I turned around and Michael was crying. "Harold, would you help me?" he asked. "I don't ever want to hurt anybody as long as I live."

"You bet I'll help you," I said, looking him square in the eyes. I then asked him for his Bible. "I'm going to write down some verses in the book of Romans and I want you to read them." I showed him where Romans was in the Bible, and then began writing: Romans 3:10, 3:23, 5:8, 6:23, 10:9-10, 10:13.

When I handed him the paper, I said, "Michael, you're intelligent. Don't let anyone tell you you're not. I want you to go to your cell and read these Scriptures. You study them. If you believe them to be true, then respond. If you don't, then don't. I'll see you next Tuesday."

On my drive home, I prayed that God would speak to him as he read the Gospel message, that he would recognize God loved him enough to send His Son to die for him, and comprehend the very personal and very eternal meaning of the last verse: "Everyone who calls on the name of the Lord will be saved."

Two days later I received a letter from Michael. "I went back to my cell on death row, opened my Bible, and read the verses you gave me," he wrote. "Then I got on my knees and I gave my heart to Jesus Christ. I am done hurting people. Would you please help me grow?" I couldn't wait a week to see him again, so I drove up the next day.

For the next few months I met with Michael every single week. Ministering to a person on death row is no easy task. These men live in a tiny world under constant pressure, and so they tend to be quite moody and high strung. Anything can upset them—a lost privilege, a minute change in routine, a letter from home, a curt word by a guard, or a note from a lawyer about their appeal. Often they explode over trivial things, but to them everything is major. I learned not to plan what I would say to these men on any given visit. I had to first see what state of mind they were in.

Michael had good weeks and bad weeks. I told him right away that there would be setbacks. "Oh no, I'm going to live for Christ. You're going to be proud of me," he'd say. The next week he'd drag into the visiting room and slump in his chair, depressed because he'd smoked dope or gotten angry at a guard.

With Michael I was committed for the long haul. I saw a lot of myself in him: both of us in prison, both on death row, both confrontive and angry, and both of us drawn to Jesus Christ by an unexpected visitor. I could tell Michael was extremely bright. He wanted to learn and grow, and so I decided to disciple him and give him the advantages I never had as a Christian while I was in prison. But it wouldn't be easy.

Shortly after his conversion, the guards were in an uproar when I arrived for my weekly visit. "We told you he was conning you," one of them said. "Bam Bam just hit a guy."

"Tell me what happened."

"He was out in the yard on exercise and hit Snake."

I knew Snake. He was a Black Muslim, a dangerous man to whom I'd briefly witnessed.

"We told you he was conning you."

"You've got it all wrong," I protested. "It's a matter of perspective. You need to recognize how far Michael's come. He only smashed one head this week. He's actually doing *better*."

The guards laughed. But the point was made.

Michael had his head down as he entered the visitor's room. "Well, I blew it," he said.

"Yeah, I heard about it. You really got into Snake."

"I'm sorry I let you down."

"No, I'm proud of you."

Michael looked up, certain that he'd heard me wrong.

"I told you this would happen. I said there would be setbacks, but you thought I was crazy. Michael, the Christian life isn't easy. It's not difficult. It's *impossible*. Only Christ could live it perfectly. You have a long way to go, and this just proves it. But

I'm proud of you. We've got you down to smashing one head a week."

"You aren't upset with me?"

"Oh no. What you did was wrong, and you need to try and make it right. But you're on course. I'm proud of you. I'm not going to turn my back on you."

It was one thing to say I believed in Michael and would help him spiritually. But he also had physical needs, and he had no money. He didn't mention his needs, but I knew what it was like. To demonstrate commitment to him, I started giving him an allowance of fifty dollars a month. With that allowance he could buy shaving supplies, toothpaste, candy, and pop from the prison store. Michael never had a father, and so I decided to try filling that role and take care of him.

Michael was slow to discuss his past. He told me a great deal about his prison life, but I knew very little about his life before he was jailed. That would take time, but I looked for opportunities to piece together his story. For example, one of his eyes seemed to wander, and I asked him about it. "Yeah, I'm blind in that eye," he explained. "I got shot in the eye with a bow and arrow when I was three years old."

If I was to piece his story together accurately, I needed to establish one rule immediately: If he lied to me and I found out, I would never come back. "You're not going to play games with me," I explained. "I have too many important things to do, and I won't waste God's money. You can tell me anything, and I'll accept you, I'll come back, and we'll work it through. If you lie to me and tell me you lied, I'll accept that. But if other people tell me you lied, I won't come back. You must be honest. If I ask you something and you don't want to answer, that's fine, up to a point. Down the road I may not accept that. But don't lie to me. Just say, 'I don't want to talk about it now.' "

I also asked that he write down his thoughts daily in a notebook. "I want you to go back and write about your life and what brought you to death row. Write down what you're thinking and feeling every day. If it's a bad day, write down who got stabbed, who got raped, how you felt. If you cried, write down why you cried.

If you laughed, write down why you laughed. You may not feel like doing this, but do it anyway." I felt this would help me to understand him better.

Michael started reading his Bible regularly, and I gave him some basic Bible studies to guide him. He'd kid me that they were too simple. "You must think I'm a first grader. *Run, Spot, Run. See the dog jump over the fence.* Come on Harold, I want something more challenging." I knew they were very basic for such an intelligent young man, but he needed to understand and apply the foundational truths of the faith.

Gradually Michael began to reveal secrets of his past, and told me about his utter hatred for homosexuals. "Before I went to prison, I'd walk up to them and smash their faces in," he said, though at first he wouldn't tell me why. Then one day he started to cry. "I was raped by the paper boy when I was three years old," he said. "My mother was married three times, and one of my stepfathers raped me. That's why I hate gays. They're sick. They're perverts. They're the scum of the earth. All they do is take advantage of young boys. Once a minister even had me stay in his home for a weekend, and had sex with me, and I hated religion because I associated Christianity with that man," he said.

Over several visits, I learned that he set his house on fire when he was five. His mother then farmed him out to a foster home, which lasted until he was placed in his first reformatory at age nine. Then he got in trouble there, and the state put him in a mental hospital. "They thought I was retarded. They gave me all kinds of psychological evaluations. They put me through drug and shock therapy. I was angry at those people. I was angry at the state. I was angry at my family. I was angry at my mother. I was angry at everybody. I wanted to bust their heads. I wanted to kill them. They kept trying to tell me what my problem was . . . *without simply asking me*."

He was released from the mental institution a few months later and bounced around between foster homes and various schools. At fifteen, he stole a car and was arrested in Pennsylvania. There he was locked up in a reformatory, but managed to escape.

On and on it went. I wept with him as I saw how all he'd

really wanted was to be loved. "I love you," I said. "I understand how much you hurt, and I'm ready to help you. You're not less of a man; you're more of a man for telling me this. I know how strong you are physically. I want you to know that if I had to choose one person on this earth to stand by me, it would be you. You're my man. But you must overcome your anger. You can't let your hurt destroy you."

Despite my gentleness, there were times I had to get tough if we were going to make any significant progress. One afternoon he entered the visitor's room spouting off about how bad everything was and how he wanted to punch someone's lights out. I listened to him for a few minutes and then said, "You know what? You need me to kick your butt."

He looked at me in shock. "What did you say?"

"I'm tired of all your crying and complaining. You've really got it pretty good. You may be sentenced to die, but a lot of people have it worse. You're not dead, yet. You've got your health. You're intelligent. I really ought to kick your butt."

"You!" He started laughing. "You kick Bam Bam's butt!" Another man was visiting with his wife in the small visiting room for death row inmates. Michael leaned over to him and said, "Hey, Johnny. This old man says he's going to kick my butt. I love it!"

I glared at him. "Let me tell you something, punk . . ."

"Punk!" Now he was howling and pounding the table.

"I'm exactly the one who can do it. You want to know why? There's no way I can beat you physically. But while you're prancing around laughing about what you can do to the old man, I'd give you one swift, well-placed kick. You could never defeat me because you're not smart enough. You're just a young dumb punk."

Michael wasn't laughing now. "You're serious, aren't you?"

"I've been through all this fighting nonsense, Michael, and have outgrown it. But you need someone to beat on you once, because that's what you've been doing to people all your life. Somebody needs to bust you and I'm exactly the one who could do it. If I wasn't a Christian, I'd do it right now."

The smile was completely gone.

"Sure, your IQ may be higher, but I'm smarter. And it's about time you quit playing games. As I've told you before, I'll go with you as far as you want. But the day you quit, I quit on you. I'm very disappointed, Michael. I don't see much growth, to tell you the truth."

"No, Harold. Please. Please don't quit on me."

"All right. Then let's get down to business. What do you want out of life?"

"I want to learn. More than anything in the world, I want an education. I'm not a high school graduate, but I'm smart. I just need a chance."

"Okay, I'll tell you what I'll do. I will enroll you in Columbia Bible College. But first I want you to complete the Bible studies I give you. If you won't do them, you won't do college work."

"There's one other thing. I would like a new trial. I want a chance to live."

I'd been waiting for the right time to talk about his case. I'd obtained the transcripts of his trial, which filled five volumes. The facts, as I saw them, were that at the age of seventeen, Michael was arrested and jailed on burglary charges. Two years later, while he was participating in a work release program, a female drug addict was raped, beaten, and stabbed to death. Michael had met the girl once, and was in the vicinity at the time of the crime. He had a criminal background, so naturally he was a prime suspect. But there seemed to be little in the way of hard evidence against him.

At our next meeting I asked a number of questions which Michael answered to my satisfaction. Finally, I asked the most important one. "Michael, I want you to tell me if you killed that girl. But before you do, I want you to know that no matter how you answer, I will still fight for your life. Because you're a Christian now, and Jesus has forgiven all of your sins, from the smallest to the biggest. But I must know the truth before we go for a new trial. After you answer me, we'll never talk about the crime again."

"Harold, I've done a lot of things in my life, and I've told you about them. I deserve to be in prison. All my life I've hated, hurt, and wanted to kill people. I honestly could handle it if I died here in the penitentiary. But I can't tell you I killed the girl, because I didn't."

"All right, I'll never ask you again. I'll get you another trial, and we're gonna win."

Working through his appeal attorney, Michael was given a new trial that December. With the cooperation of his trial attorney, I raised $5,000 to secure expert witnesses and pay their expenses. Based on the evidence we obtained, I felt confident that Michael would win his release.

Meanwhile, Michael breezed through the Navigator's study I'd given him and memorized the verses that went with it. Again he pleaded for something more challenging. So I enrolled him in Columbia Bible College for a special thirty-hour program of correspondence Bible courses. He eagerly buried himself in the work.

During the trial, a forensic expert testified that Michael could not have raped the woman, based on extensive analysis of blood and semen. Michael had met the woman once, when he stopped by to visit a boy who lived next door. The boy wasn't home, so he asked the woman to deliver a note, which she did. Twelve days later she was found dead. Based on that contact, Michael's palm print inside the house where he'd written the note, his lousy record, and his lack of a good alibi, Michael was nailed.

But there was additional evidence that wasn't checked. There were numerous fingerprints all over the house where the crime occurred, but police never identified them. Another man had recently beaten the woman during an argument, but he was never investigated. Police apparently believed it was an open and shut case. As the saying goes, where there's smoke, there's fire. Unfortunately, there was smoke all around Michael, but somebody else set the fire.

After a four-day trial, the jury returned with a verdict of "not guilty" for the rape charges, "guilty" for the murder charge, and a recommendation that Michael's death sentence be changed to life imprisonment.

I was shocked. It seemed obvious to me that the woman was raped and murdered by the same man. This was a tragedy. At that moment, I was ready to trade places with Michael and serve the rest of his sentence.

But Michael had a different perspective. He looked at me with tears in his eyes and said, "We won, Harold. We won!"

"No, no we lost. I'm sorry."

"No, Harold, we won!"

"How can you say that?"

"I'm free from the sentence of death. Now I have my whole life ahead of me to study the Word and a witness inside the prison. All I asked for was my life. And now that I have it, I intend to live for Christ."

I looked at him with a feeling of awe. There could no longer be any doubt about the genuineness of this man's conversion. He was learning a lesson about faith that I couldn't comprehend. I was dejected; he was victorious. At that moment, I determined I would stand by him as long as I lived. He would have every opportunity to grow and become all God wanted him to be.

Michael was immediately transferred off death row to another prison and then back to the main population at Central Correctional Institute, the state prison in Columbia, South Carolina. He quickly completed his correspondence Bible courses, passed his high school equivalency exam, and was eventually admitted to the University of South Carolina. The professors came and taught him and several other inmates at the prison. I arranged to pay for all of his schooling, including tuition, books, and miscellaneous expenses.

But there were setbacks. Arrangements were made to transfer Michael to another prison so he could be in an environment so people didn't know about his old reputation. During transport he was handcuffed between two other inmates. What Michael didn't know was that these two men were smuggling a gun into the new prison, and as soon as they arrived they took a hostage. The incident was over quickly, but all three of them were immediately locked in the hole.

Michael was allowed one phone call, and he made it to me. "I didn't do anything," he protested.

I had a sinking feeling that all my work was going for naught. I called the warden, who refused to discuss the issue. "Is he guilty of something?" I asked.

"Well, we're investigating. I can't tell you."

"Wait a minute. If he's been charged with something, I need to know what it is. If he hasn't done anything, set him free."

The warden wouldn't budge, so I went to the corrections commissioner and exerted some pressure. "Sir, all I'm asking is that if Michael Godwin is guilty, you charge him. If he's not, move him back where he belongs."

The next day Michael was transferred back to the prison in Columbia. Though he was innocent of any wrongdoing, I was tired, and I told Michael so during my next visit. "I'm not going to bat for you again," I said. "You must learn to stand on your own two feet. You've got to learn to manage your life. They're waiting for you to blow it one more time so they can bust you."

With his head bowed, he said, "I'm sorry. It won't ever happen again."

"Do you understand why you got in trouble? I know why, because I was the same way. You're very intimidating and hardheaded. You go right up to the line, but then you don't stop. You go one step too far."

"You're right. I understand now."

Loving Michael was hard work. With my encouragement, he called me collect several times a week. Once I checked my phone bills and counted more than 500 collect calls over several years. Often those calls came at times when I didn't feel like talking. And they cost a lot of money. More than once I wanted to desert him, but then I'd think, "I can't do that, any more than a father can drop his son." The analogy was appropriate. I could imagine that being a good father was just as hard and equally frustrating.

Michael progressed rapidly through his studies, and on August 16, 1986, he completed his bachelor of arts degree with a major in English and a minor in government and international studies. He had a near-perfect 3.85 grade point average, even though he worked a prison job as a plumber and electrician. He was named to the National Dean's List and the Gamma Beta Phi national honor society. In 1986 he was chosen one of the top ten young men of America in South Carolina. Only ten are selected, and he was chosen again in 1987 for the second year in a row. When he told me he wanted to continue his education and get his masters degree in counseling, I arranged for him to do that through Luther Rice Seminary. He completed that degree one year later, with a perfect 4.0 grade point average. In those achievements, I saw the other side of being a father—the pride of a son who's done well.

On my visit to him following his graduation from the University of South Carolina, I said, "You know what, son?"

"Yeah, Daddy?"

"I believe your allowance needs to be upped a little bit. You've earned it, and Daddy's proud of you."

"Well, thank you Daddy. What did you have in mind?"

"How about a hundred dollars?"

"All right! Man that will really help out. Now I can quit my job and concentrate solely on my studies."

We talked often about what he wanted to do with his life. Even in prison, his hands were full. He was a witness to the inmates and guards. In fact, the officers who once hated him now loved him. One day he heard a commotion and discovered two guards in a brawl with several inmates. Michael tore in and broke up the fight. Then he administered first aid to one guard and carried the other to the infirmary.

"I look at the guards as people now," he said to me after that incident. "As a Christian I've gotten to know them and realize they are people doing a job. I'm not angry at them anymore."

Michael also reached out to young people. The orphanage where he spent some time as a teenager bussed their residents to the prison so he could speak to them. He offered to write and send helpful cassettes to any kids who were on drugs or having any problems.

After I spoke at a school in Arkansas, a young girl came up to me and said, "Sir, can I write to an inmate?" I gave her Michael's name and they began corresponding. She told him about how she was involved in drugs and alcohol and wanted to drop out of school, leave home. Michael counseled her not to do that. He encouraged her to be courageous, to claim the promises of Scripture, and fight through her problems.

One evening Michael called me, and he was distraught. "I've blown it. I've lost that girl."

"What do you mean?" I asked.

"She wrote and told me she was leaving home and quitting school because she hated her mom and dad. I made a cassette and sent it to her, and I was very hard on her. I said, 'Go ahead, drop out of school! Leave home! Let me tell you what is going to happen. You'll become a drug addict, a prostitute. You'll wreck your life. You need to go home and ask your parents to forgive you.' Harold, I was too hard on her. She's stopped writing and I haven't heard from her in a month."

"I'm proud of you. You did the right thing. I know it was hard. You're eager for her to follow the Lord and obey Him. You loved her enough to tell her the truth. But sometimes people choose not to listen."

Two years later, Michael finally got a letter from the girl. "Mr. Godwin, I want to thank for your advice," she began. "I did what you said. I went to my parents and asked for forgiveness. Things aren't perfect but we're learning to communicate. By the way, I graduated as the valedictorian in my high school, and I'm in college now."

There was no doubt in my mind that God had a great plan for Michael. I told him that after he obtained his master's degree I would do everything legally possible to obtain his release from prison so he could work on a Ph.D. I'd never heard of any inmate achieving what this man had while still behind bars. I realized that it would be an adjustment coming out of prison, just as it was for me. He told me the first thing he wanted to do was enjoy a triple decker hamburger at Wendy's, followed by a large order of fries at McDonald's, and topped by a Big Gulp at Hardees. He'd seen them all advertised on TV, but had never been in any of these restaurants. Of course, learning to eat at fast food eateries would be fun, but there would be other more difficult adjustments if he merged back into society. I was ready to do whatever it took to help him make the transition. Here was a man who had maimed people for years. Now he wanted to counsel young people and help them travel the straight and narrow road that leads to eternal life.

Of course, there was a chance Michael might not be released, and we had to honestly confront that possibility. One day, I asked him point blank, "Michael, you've spent sixteen of your twenty-six years in reformatories and prisons. You have a life sentence and could easily spend another twenty years in prison before you're eligible for parole. Today, would you trade your relationship with Jesus Christ for your freedom, so you could walk out of this prison?"

He didn't know the question was coming, but never hesitated in his answer. "I would rather have the penalty of death and spend the rest of my life knowing I would die in the electric chair than give up my commitment to Jesus Christ," he said. "I love Him with all my heart, and nothing in life has given me more joy than my personal relationship with the Lord."

Michael's answer demonstrated that he knew what tough faith was all about. It had been refined in the crucible of harsh prison life. Meanwhile, God was not finished molding me. I was about to learn another lesson in faith through a trial more terrible than my worst prison nightmare.

Chapter Nine

IT AIN'T MUCH
OF A JOB....

It was April 1984, and I was lying in a hospital bed, still groggy from pain killers after an operation to remove a knot on my neck. A doctor had just told me the bad news. The knot was malignant. He and two other physicians had discovered cancer behind my left ear, in my sinuses, tongue, throat, and lymph nodes. With treatment, my physicians said, I might live three more years.

Thus began one of the toughest periods of my life. I'd faced many killers at Georgia State Penitentiary. I'd fought for my life at great odds and survived. But this was different. This murderer was as tough as they come and invisible. I couldn't just beat him to the ground, and then walk away confident that I'd won the fight.

My experience with illness was minimal; I couldn't remember ever being sick. I'd spent some time in the prison hospital after an inmate split open my head and it took thirty-nine stitches to sew me back together. The pain of cancer didn't scare me, but there were so many other unknowns. How would my friends react? What would I look like after treatments? Could I continue my work speaking to kids and prisoners? How much would the cancer treatments cost? How long would I be sick? How would I react to a slow, painful death? Would I have to die alone?

Fortunately I had one role model. I'd watched my friend Russell Moore die of cancer while I was in Bible school. Each time I visited him in the hospital, I did something crazy, such as feel around his bed and exclaim, "Good night, there's a leg missing! Russell, where is it? Your doctor has told you to take your medicine and get plenty of rest. But you're not following his instructions, because your leg's missing!"

Russell would burst out laughing. "You're crazy, Harold," he'd say. He was right; I was crazy. But I believe my warped humor helped him. Once he told me he especially liked my visits because I wasn't quiet and self-conscious around his hospital bed as were most of his other friends. Perhaps by accident I'd learned that joking and laughter was a healthy way to face the problem honestly, and it opened the door for Russell to discuss his feelings. That's not to say the visits were easy. I watched him spit up blood and parts of a tumor, and the sight made me nauseous. I saw him shrivel to half his original weight and struggle for every breath. But his testimony never wavered. To the end, he was faithful to the Lord, and his last words to me before he died were, "You're a loyal friend, Harold, but never forget this: It's loyalty to Christ that counts."

Now it was my turn to face cancer. Other than Russell, I had no example to guide me in this moment on the brink of life and death. My first decision was to laugh whenever possible. I saw humor as being one of God's ways to help me cope with the heavy load of pain and uncertainty. That didn't mean turning on the TV and listening to some comedian's litany of sexist or racial jokes. Rather, I tried to see the natural humor around me, and to laugh at myself. Humor had certainly helped me through prison and other difficult times. Somehow, I now had to try to find the humor in my illness.

When the doctor left my room after delivering the bad news, my close friend Randy Gradishar, then a linebacker for the Denver Broncos, walked up to my bed, squeezed my hand, and started blubbering, "I love you. You're my closest friend. You've helped me grow so much spiritually. I don't understand why you have to die. Of all people, Harold, why you?"

I didn't have any great theological answers. All I could say was, "Randy, I've been going around all these years telling people how they ought to live. Now maybe God wants me to show them how to die." I paused and gave him a painful smile. "It ain't much of a job, but somebody's got to do it. And it might as well be me."

Up until six months before my operations, I was too poor to afford any health or life insurance. Thankfully, I was finally able to get both just before I needed them. I was grateful to God for that, because my medical bills skyrocketed to heights that made me dizzy just thinking about them.

As soon as I was released from the hospital, the doctors on my case recommended that I consult another physician, Dr. David Devonshire. "He's taught us everything we know," they said. Three good doctors already had given up on me, and I wasn't sure how a fourth opinion, regardless of how smart the man was, could change my prognosis. Nevertheless, I agreed to see him.

I had a week to think about my situation before that appointment. Despite my upbeat statement to Randy Gradishar, I needed encouragement. The words of the Apostle Paul in Philippians 1:21 came to mind: "For to me, to live is Christ and to die is gain." Could I honestly say that? Paul had the right attitude, but then he was an apostle. I was just an ugly old ex-con. Nevertheless, I did my best to take his words to heart. He was able to say in Romans 8:18, "I consider that our present sufferings are not worth comparing with the glory that will be revealed in us." To me that meant one thing: Whatever pain I might have to endure would last only a short time in comparison to eternity. Still, I wanted to prepare, if that was possible, for whatever lay ahead so that my life or death might also honor God. The only place I knew to find such input was the Bible.

It seemed natural to go to the book of Job. If there was ever a man who was justified in asking why he was afflicted with sorrow and suffering, Job was that man. He was one of the choicest among God's people, an upright man who feared the Lord. In addition to being one of the wealthiest people around, he was also a diligent family man. God Himself said He had no reason to afflict Job. So why did he suffer overwhelming adversity?

As I looked for the answer to that question, I couldn't help noticing the basic message of this book: the sovereignty of God. God was in full control of Job's life, and likewise, I knew He was in control of every situation in my life. Nothing happened to me by chance or accident. Job's trials only deepened his faith and drew him closer to God. He never questioned the sovereignty of God, and so, as a Christian, neither could I.

Job's response to the loss of his possessions, his family, and his health was incredible: "Naked I came from my mother's womb, and naked I will depart. The Lord gave and the Lord has taken away; may the name of the Lord be praised" (Job 1:21). Even more amazing was that throughout the tragedy, Job did not sin. How was it possible for him to respond that way? Could I continue to bow and worship in the darkest hour of my life?

Job didn't have a lot of encouragement in his trial. His wife advised him to "curse God and die." Three of his friends "ministered" to him by saying he was to blame for all of his troubles. So ultimately, Job suffered alone.

I thought a great deal about these words of wisdom from Job to his accusing friends:

> But he knows the way that I take;
> when he has tested me, I will come forth as gold.
> My feet have closely followed his steps;
> I have kept to his way without turning aside.
> I have not departed from the commands of his lips;
> I have treasured the words of his mouth more
> than my daily bread.
> But he stands alone, and who can oppose him?
> He does whatever he pleases.
>   (Job 23:10-13)

That was tough faith, and I knew I would need all of it that I could muster for this crisis. In effect, Job said he would not give up on God, because God had allowed the troubles and knew what was best for him. Whatever was in store, my afflictions were for my own good. I would seek God first, and allow Him to do His will in my situation. Job had even said, "Though He slay me, yet will I hope in Him" (Job 13:15). If Job could say that and mean it, so could I.

That was my perspective as I headed to my appointment with Dr. Devonshire, accompanied by four friends. The doctor entered the examination room carrying a long tube with a light on the end of it. As he sprayed my throat with an anesthetic, he told me he'd studied all my reports and X-rays, and knew a great deal about me even if I knew nothing about him. As he talked, I could see my friends peeking around the door.

"Can my friends come in?" I asked Dr. Devonshire.

"Sure, if you don't care."

I waved them all in, and they stood against the wall like eager-eyed school boys about to see a biology teacher dissect a frog. The doctor inserted the tube into my nostrils and tore through a membrane leading into the sinus cavities in my head. The sudden pain was so intense I nearly passed out. He then threaded the lighted tube around inside my head, and from there down into my throat. Tears clouded my eyes as he shifted the tube around, scoping out my interior passages.

As he peered through the outer end, Dr. Devonshire dictated a running commentary of his sight-seeing tour while an assistant took notes. I didn't understand a thing he was saying, but I kept thinking, "Lord, he's going to pull that tube out and tell me my future." Regardless of the impressive diplomas hanging on his wall, I knew he couldn't tell me anything that I didn't already know: I was dying.

Finally he pulled out his scope, cleaned it off and looked at me for a long moment. "I suppose you want to know how long you're going to live," he said matter-of-factly.

"Well the thought had occurred to me," I responded rubbing my nose. I could still feel the tube inside my head even though it had been removed.

"Some people have heart attacks and die; some people have cancer," he began. "*You* have cancer. And you'll need a lot of luck and prayer in the weeks ahead." He glanced over at my friends, who were now shifting uneasily on their feet. "I'm rec-ommending that you be treated with radiation, the maximum dosage, starting tomorrow. I know the best doctor in town, and will call him. He will treat you at St. Joseph's Hospital every day for the next two months. When the treatment is completed, take thirty days off to recuperate. And then, if you're alive, come back and see me."

On the ride home with my friends, nobody wanted to talk. Finally I spoke up. "This radiologist, he can't help me. He can treat me, but if I'm healed it will be because of Christ. I'll fight the cancer to the best of my ability. I'll listen to the doctors and do what they say, because they are a gift from God. But the final decision as to whether I live or die is out of their hands."

During the ride, I remembered a story I'd heard about a young boy who held a small bird in his hand and tried to trick a wise old hermit.

"Hey, you old coot," the boy said. "If you think you're so smart, tell me whether the bird I've got in my hands is dead or alive."

The old man looked at the boy, and then looked at the young hands cupped tightly around the bird. He knew that if he said it was alive, the boy would simply break its neck. If he said it was dead, the boy would release the bird to fly away.

"Young man, it's as God wills. The answer is in your hands."

The next day I entered St. Joseph's Hospital, masking my fear of the unknown with a smile and bravado. The future was as God wills. When I met the radiation specialist, I looked him in the eye and said, "I want you to know you can level with this patient. I don't know how you determine the amount of radiation you give somebody, but I want the biggest dose possible. My heart can take it. So turn that machine on high, because we're going to kill those cancer cells. And if we don't, it's because Jesus Christ doesn't want them killed. So give me the straight scoop. Level with me. I want to know everything that's going on."

The therapist explained that each day he would paint marks on my head and neck to indicate where the technician was to shoot the radiation. "It won't hurt at first," he assured me. "Later the skin on your face will turn pink, then brown, and will eventually peel. You'll also probably experience some nausea."

"Will I lose my hair?"

"No, but you might want to get your teeth pulled, at least any bad ones, because you'll lose them anyway."

"I can't do that. I've worked too hard to save them."

"As you wish. Other than that, you should be able to live normally. You can go to work, do whatever you'd normally do, as long as you feel up to it."

"Will this affect my appetite?"

"Not at all. Eat three meals a day. You'll need them."

With those assurances, a nurse ushered me into a little room, where I stripped to the waist and donned a hospital gown. I was then taken to the treatment area and placed atop a large table. My head was taped to the table, and the machine aligned to the marks on my face where the radiation would be blasted. Then the lights were turned off, and I was left in the room alone.

When the machine clicked on, it sounded like a jet airplane taking off. I had been told it wouldn't hurt, and the actual blast of radiation didn't. But while the machine was on the hair on my stomach stood straight up, as if I was being jolted with electricity. The pain came later.

The first few days weren't too bad. I immediately bought a WaterPik and a new supply of toothbrushes to help preserve my teeth. I was determined not to lose a single tooth and began brushing ten to twelve times a day, using a different toothbrush each time. I still remembered the years in solitary confinement when I'd flossed with a thread from my shirt and massaged my gums daily.

By the end of the first week of radiation treatments, I was feeling a lump in my throat that made it difficult to swallow. I mentioned it to the radiologist, but he said there was nothing to worry about. A few days later the lump felt like a baseball, and I found it almost impossible to swallow. Again the doctor ignored my complaint. "Just eat normally," he said.

But I couldn't eat at all; it was too painful. Sores and blisters developed inside my mouth. I vomited my guts out. Ten years of imprisonment were nothing compared to the physical agony of trying to rid my body of this disease. Fortunately, there were friends around to lift my spirits. Randy Gradishar flew his wife, Janet, and kids out. They stayed two weeks in Atlanta, taking me to and from the hospital and cleaning my apartment. Jim Ryan, another linebacker with the Broncos, and his lovely wife, Sara, stayed nearby during their honeymoon to be with me and drive me to the doctor's office. I had planned to be in their wedding until my illness dictated otherwise.

One day I received a phone call from the University of Alabama. The secretary was calling to get directions from the airport to my apartment on behalf of Ray Perkins, then head football coach at the university, and later named head coach at Tampa Bay. I had spoken several times to his football team and we had developed a friendship. The next day, Ray arrived at my apartment shortly after I'd had my radiation treatment. I was feeling exhausted, but I was encouraged by his words: "You're tough. You're made of good stuff. You're a winner, and you can lick this. God's not through with you yet." It was a tremendous lift, knowing this busy man took time off from his hectic schedule to fly over from another state just to encourage an old ex-con with cancer.

Not everyone was such an encouragement. Some had to visit just out of curiosity. Though they probably meant well, they didn't help. One friend was waiting in my apartment when I arrived home from my daily treatment. He took one look at me and exclaimed, "My God, you're dying!" He grabbed me and started praying, "Lord, I love Harold more than anyone on earth. Take the cancer out of his body, and put it in mine—"

"Lord, give it to him," I interrupted. "Give it to him right now!"

My friend jumped, and the look on his face told me he really didn't mean what he'd prayed. "Hey, I've had it long enough," I said, trying to smile. "Go ahead and try it for a while."

I was grateful that there were others who stood by me, cried, and suffered as I suffered. It wasn't easy for me to accept their help. I'd always been a giver and found it hard to receive. Many times I refused help because I wanted to be left alone. Perhaps because of the years spent in solitary confinement, I felt more comfortable fighting this battle without any witnesses.

I was aware that my appearance caused people to notice me. Little kids stared as if I was some sort of carnival freak. This was because there were indelible paint marks on my face and neck, indicating target areas for the radiation. Elsewhere on my face, large spots of skin looked like they'd been cooked over a barbecue pit. When I felt the energy, I'd go out, but the gawking was irritating. With embarrassment, I realized that for years, I, too, had stared at people who looked different.

One afternoon I stopped at a motel near my apartment to make reservations for some friends who were coming to Atlanta. I noticed a group in the lobby staring at me. When I looked square at them, they turned away, so I walked over. "Hey, would you all like to know what's wrong with me?"

"Well, yeah, what is wrong with you?" said one man, a little nervous but obviously glad to have his curiosity satisfied.

"I'm an Indian chief, and this is part of my makeup. I entertain at parties. You ought to see me sometime; I do a great war dance."

The man gave me a funny look, so I said, "No, really, I have cancer. But don't feel sorry for me. I'm doing pretty good."

"You act as though nothing is wrong."

"Well, nothing is wrong. I just have cancer, but I'm going to lick it. I know Jesus Christ as my Lord and Savior, and He's going to see me through it. But even if I don't make it, I'm going to a better place."

The man shook his head and said, "I've never seen anybody with an attitude like that."

"You aren't a Christian, are you?"

"Can't say that I am."

"That explains it. You see, if you had a personal relationship with Christ, you would understand. Without Him, I couldn't handle this at all. I'd have no hope."

It felt good to leave those people with a statement that might cause them to think about the Lord. Even in my illness, I could glorify God. But as the effects of my treatments worsened, I spent less time outside my apartment. All of my energy was sapped just to make the daily twenty-two-mile round trip to the hospital and endure the treatments. My physical condition deteriorated rapidly. At times I felt so sick that I prayed for death. Not only could I not eat, it became unbearable to drink even an ounce of cold water. The pain was so bad that doctors shot and fed me every kind of painkilling drug imaginable, including marijuana in pill form. I was dehydrated. I couldn't sleep and I had nightmares even with my eyes open. At times, the only thing I could grasp was that God was right there beside me, day after painful day. He was there when it hurt, and when it kept on hurting and hurting and hurting. . . .

One godly woman became a Florence Nightingale to me. She was Julia Williams, wife of one of my closest friends from the three years I'd attended Guilford College before going to prison. They were with me when I had my operation and first learned I had cancer. Several times during the following weeks, Julia flew over from Raleigh, North Carolina, with her husband's permission and cared for me. At times I was so sick I begged her to leave so she wouldn't see my agony. Instead of leaving, she'd bring a bucket of ice water and put cold packs on my burning face. I noticed her tears as the steam rose from my face when she removed a cloth and replaced it with a fresh one from the ice bucket.

Julia was particularly concerned about my inability to eat or drink. I was rapidly losing weight and strength. She bought some cans of Sustacal and Nutrament and served them to me in a glass with a straw to force some nutrition into my body. It took thirty minutes to drink just one eight ounce can, and Julia had to coach me all the way. "Just take another sip; you don't have much more to go," she'd say. Some days she had to trick me into taking enough sips so I wouldn't die of malnutrition.

Finally it became obvious that I wasn't getting enough food. My body was dehydrated, and Julia drove me back to the hospital so they could feed me intravenously. However, the treatments at times seemed to be worse than the disease, and I was growing increasingly weary. I begged the doctor to stop the treatments. "This is killing me," I said. "Please, please stop."

"We're so close. We can't stop now," he argued. But it was obvious my body simply could not take any more without a rest, so it was agreed I would take a break for one week.

There were times I wondered if all this agony was worth it. Sometimes all I could do was lie in my bed trying to comprehend how God was working. I knew no matter what happened or how long my life lasted, God wanted the glory. But this seemed like a horrible way to glorify God. I thought about how, in the previous year, I'd spoken 368 times in schools, prisons, and churches. In February, just two months before my surgery, Focus on the Family had aired a two-part tape of my message to Apex High School in Raleigh, North Carolina, and it drew a record response of more than fifteen thousand letters. Opportunities were opening up for me all over the country. I had speaking engagements booked several years ahead. So why was I sick now? Why was I dying of cancer? Why were doctors saying the end was near when my work was finally beginning to blossom?

As I lay in bed trying to make sense of it all, I thought, *Wait a minute, this isn't fair. I love God and have tried to serve Him. He's my Lord and Savior. So, why me?*

In a flash I sensed God's answer within me, in terms I could understand: *Hey Dummy, why not you? Just because you did ten years in prison—which, for the record, was your own fault—do you think you should be exempt from other problems? Do you feel you deserve a medal, or two weeks vacation where you can sin all you want? Do you want people to think, "Poor Harold, he's gone through so much"? Let Me tell you something. You are just like everybody else, and won't get any special treatment from Me. That doesn't mean I don't love you. I love you enough to have allowed Christ to suffer an awful death on your behalf. Don't ever forget that. And while you're at it, don't forget that I want the glory for your life—no matter what.*

I felt like Job probably did after God was through with him. God never told Job the "whys" of his suffering. He simply revealed Himself. That was all I needed—to know God in a deeper way. As I got a clearer picture of who God was, I could trust Him more. In those bleak hours, I prayed, *Lord, this is the*

*most difficult experience of my life, but my hope is still in You.
I thank You for the tremendous pain, because I don't know what
else to do. I'm leaning on You.*

It was shortly after that when I saw these words in Psalm
118:17-18. I had Julia read them aloud to me:

> I will not die but live,
> and will proclaim what the Lord had done.
> The Lord has chastened me severely,
> but he has not given me over to death.

On the day my treatments resumed at St. Joseph's Hospital,
my doctor told me about a young twenty-eight-year-old woman
named Linda O'Malley who had the same type of cancer I did.
He said she was just starting her treatment, and was feeling
depressed. "Would you mind speaking to her?" he asked. "She's
in the waiting room."

When I first saw her, I was struck by her beauty. She weighed
a petite 110 pounds, and her long brown hair curled atop her
shoulders. Her eyes were bright, and her smile warm.

After a moment of small talk, during which I learned she was
a flight attendant, I asked if she was a Christian. I wanted to
know, because either one of us could be dead within a short
period of time. Cancer patients come . . . and before you know
it, they are gone. I'd become attached to one old man whose
appointment was close to mine at 10:15 every morning. I noticed
he wasn't there one day when I came in, so I asked the nurse
about him. "Mr. Johnson didn't make it," she said quietly. I
didn't know if somebody would have my slot the following week,
or if Linda would be around the next month. So I got right to
the point, and asked if she'd ever invited Jesus Christ into her
heart.

Linda smiled and said, "Yes, I was saved four years ago.
Another flight attendant told me about Christ, and that same night
I trusted Him as my Savior."

"I'm told we have the same type of cancer," I said. "And since
I've been at this a few weeks longer, I want you to know the

treatment is a piece of cake. With God's help you can lick this thing. Whatever happens, please don't be bitter at the Lord. He's all the hope we have, and He will see us through this."

She smiled, but was too choked up to talk. I understood. When you're young, death isn't something you've thought a lot about. The prospect of dying before you've really lived can be terrible.

"If I can do anything for you, please let me know."

"Thank you," she said. When I came out after the treatment, Linda was gone. I looked for her on subsequent visits as well, but we never crossed paths. Finally, I asked the receptionist about her. She said Linda had lost so much weight that treatments had to be stopped. She had gone to Birmingham, Alabama, to be with her parents. I understood, without the nurse having to say it, that Linda had gone home to die.

Shortly after that, I asked the radiologist, "What are my odds of surviving?"

Without hesitating, he answered, "Thirty-two percent."

"How do you determine that?"

"Based on all the patients I've treated with the same type of cancer you have, and the number who have survived. It's thirty-two percent."

"Wow, thank God!"

"Excuse me, I don't think you understand—"

"Oh, I understand. You've got to realize those are the best odds I've ever had. When I was in prison, my odds weren't that good."

"You are amazing," the doctor said with a chuckle.

The doctor thought I had a great attitude, but he didn't see the emotions that churned underneath my happy-go-lucky exterior. Encounters with people like Linda only intensified those feelings. Few people saw the fear, bordering at times on panic. I was scared. I had to constantly remind myself of Christ's words, "Fear not." He was with me, but fear wore many disguises: anxiety, doubt, indecision, superstition, withdrawal, loneliness, worry, inferiority, hesitance, depression, and shyness. Sometimes my fear was so great that I feared my *fears*. The only relief was to go to the Lord in prayer, and so often I waited much too long to do that.

Only as I poured by heart out to God did I experience any sense of His peace.

Doctors had tried to prepare me for the physical pain I endured. But no one told me about the emotional trauma that cancer and radiation treatments produce. Many times, all I could do was cry, and that was somehow comforting. As it is said, "Tears, like fallen rain, wash the windows of our soul."

Not all my tears were shed in the solitude of my apartment. One day at the cleaners, the lady behind the counter asked me about the markings on my face. When I told her about my radiation treatments she nodded. She told me that two years earlier she'd lost her seventeen-year-old son to a brain tumor. As I listened to her talk, I realized that many others were suffering their own private pain far worse than mine. For the first time, I recognized people who were genuinely hurting. They'd always been around me; I'd simply never seen them.

Though at times I felt as if God had forsaken me and left me alone in my miseries, I had to remind myself that He was always there. He promised in Hebrews 13:5 never to forsake us, so I knew He would never turn His back on me. I could trust Him. God did not leave us alone in the midst of our sorrow and despair, but provided a way for us to go *through* them.

That truth was reinforced by a wonderful friend who understood suffering. Right after the last radiation treatment, Becky called and told me she and Tonya were coming to visit me in Atlanta. I was sitting up for them as they arrived. These two special women cried, and held me in their arms, and told me they loved me.

"You look so thin," said Tonya.

"I've dropped a couple of pounds."

"How many?" she wanted to know.

I'd actually lost ninety-two pounds, but I didn't want to tell her. "Hey, I've really improved. You should have seen me last week."

For a while I'd lost touch with Becky after she remarried. I wasn't sure how her new husband would feel about our relationship, so I'd purposely stayed away. Becky occasionally dropped me notes, but I didn't answer them. There was a tinge of sadness in that, but I felt God had fulfilled His plan for us.

Then one day I spoke at a prayer breakfast in her town, and both she and Max were there. After my talk, Max approached, "That's the greatest testimony I've ever heard," he said, and he then invited me to come and stay at their home any time. It meant a great deal to see how much Max loved Becky and Tonya. And now he was letting them come and visit me when I was in need.

After Tonya cheered me up by relaying some corny jokes she'd heard in school, I looked over at her mother. "You know, Becky," I began, "a lot of people ask, 'Why is this tragedy happening to me?' Or, 'Is God punishing me for some horrible sin in my life?' The anguish of cancer has led me to those same inevitable questions. Sometimes God provides answers. Then again, we may never know why God allowed the death of your husband and son, or my illness."

Becky nodded silently. And then she told me she saw a difference in me. "I can tell you've matured spiritually. It's written all over you. You've developed a stronger relationship with the Lord."

"That's because I've been in a unique position: flat on my back. All of my props have been removed. Even friends and family disappeared. On the surface, that's not an enviable position. Yet I've found that when God is all I have, He is all I want."

"I know what you mean," Becky said. "When I reached the point where I wanted God's will above all else, whether single or married, that's when I began to overcome my grief."

"I'm just glad I read the book of Job before I started radiation. That helped me gain the perspective I needed. And since then, the Scriptures have come alive for me. I think I've learned more from God's Word these past few weeks than all the previous years I've been a Christian."

As Becky and Tonya prepared to leave at the end of the day, Becky gave my hand a tender squeeze. "Harold, I want to thank you for all you've done for me," she said. "God knew I needed

a strong man to help me through that time. You were God's man,
and I thank you."

I was moved by that as I hugged these two wonderful women.
They were pulling for me now, just as I'd pulled for them when
they were hurting. Love had come full circle.

I would need that love in the coming days. The radiation treatments were finally completed. Unfortunately, I felt horrible. My
skin was peeling. My mouth and throat were so blistered and swollen I could hardly swallow. My saliva glands and taste buds had
been destroyed. It was time to rest and recover before I went back
to Dr. Devonshire to learn if the treatments had done their job.

Chapter Ten

BLACKOUT

It was one o'clock on a muggy July afternoon. Radiation treatments had ended a few days earlier. I was alone in my apartment, sitting at my desk in the living room, surrounded by a few precious items: a photograph of football great Bear Bryant, which he'd autographed and sent one month before he died; my dog-eared Bible; shelves of books, some I'd read and some I hadn't yet found the time to read; and stacks of letters waiting to be answered.

I tried to ignore the fiery pain in my mouth as I studied the Bible, but my head began to ache after I'd read just a few verses. Then it *really* began to ache. I felt winded, as if I'd just run a mile full-tilt, and I couldn't concentrate. Nothing made sense. I rubbed my forehead, but the pain went too deep.

I set my Bible down and tried to find a comfortable position in my broad wooden chair. I leaned back, and stared at several wall hangings: a cross-stitching by Julia, my Florence Nightingale, of the four Bible verses—1 John 1:9, Romans 6:23, 1 Peter 2:24, and Revelation 3:20—which God had used to lead me to Christ; an embroidered saying, "It's loyalty to Christ that counts"; a cross-stitched maxim, "Children's lives are like twigs—they grow in the direction they are bent"; and the twenty-five-dollar check given me upon my release from Georgia State Penitentiary.

I was used to having dizzy spells whenever I stood up, but suddenly, as I sat, the walls began to spin. I squeezed the armrests of my chair, but the walls and pictures kept spinning. I felt like

136

I was on a fast merry-go-round that had slipped a cog and was about to rocket off its axis. It was as though I was caught in a horror movie. Suddenly my head crashed against my desk and everything went black.

When I regained consciousness, my head was lying on some envelopes scattered across the desk. Opening my eyes, I saw only a blurry darkness. Several minutes passed before I realized where I was and who I was. But my world remained black. My hands groped across the top of the desk, sending envelopes flying. Suddenly my heart began lurching out of control in my chest, and my arms started shaking violently. The shaking spread across my entire body. My heart felt ready to explode. My pulse galloped in my head, and slammed against the inside of my chest like a rapid-fire cannon. Sweat poured off my body. My hair was soaked. Streams of perspiration coursed down my back.

With great effort I grabbed my chest, unsure of what to do next. Then the thought struck: *I am dying!* As my heart bucked and lurched, I slid out of my chair, got on my hands and knees, and began to crawl toward the bathroom. My brain screamed for water. Somehow I had to cool down my head. Still unable to see, I crawled across the living room, through my bedroom and into the bathroom. I pulled myself across the linoleum, and leaned over the commode. Fortunately a towel was lying nearby; I sloshed it around inside the toilet and plastered it over my face.

Then I crawled to my bed, pulled myself up onto the mattress and sprawled across it on my back. My chest was heaving, and the perspiration continued pouring. I was blind to everything. I knew my heart had to burst. I tried to hold it, to take deep even breaths, but that didn't help.

This was it. Death was just moments away. The only thing I could think to do was reach out to God. "Father, I love you," I said aloud, gasping for breath. "I want to thank You for saving me. If it's Your will that I die right now, take me home. I want to be with You. But I don't feel ready to die yet. I still want to live. I want to see my mother, my family, my friends. I want to tell more people about Your love. I want to share about the amazing things You've done in my life. However, I accept Your will, even if at this moment it means death. I just ask that You take care of my dear mother. Keep Your hand on her life."

Having said that prayer, I closed my eyes and waited for my heart to lurch one final time. Instead, at that moment, an amazing thing happened. My heart stopped pounding and returned to its normal beat. The breaths I'd struggled for came easier. I still felt incredible pain in my head and chest, but a peace surrounded me which surpassed understanding. God was not calling me home yet.

My body continued shaking, and my vision remained black. As I kept perfectly still, I began to see pools of light swim before me, presumably coming from my bedroom window. Within the light pools, I slowly began to differentiate colors. Splashes of greens and blues circled in front of me. I adjusted the wet cloth on my head, but was careful to keep movement to a minimum.

Suddenly the phone rang. I tried to ignore it, but the ring was insistent. I reached over to the nightstand and groped for the receiver. Slowly I brought it up to my ear and mumbled a groggy hello.

"Harold, what's wrong?" the voice said at the other end. It was Bobby Richardson, calling from South Carolina. "I can't explain this, but I felt led to call and check up on you."

"Bobby, I just fainted," I said. "I'm still having problems, but I'll be all right. Would you mind calling me back in a little while?"

"Are you alone?" he asked.

"Yes."

"I'm going to call an ambulance."

"No, Bobby, I feel better."

"An ambulance could be there in minutes."

"No, I'll be all right."

"Okay, I'll call back in thirty minutes to check on you."

I tried to sit up, but the room started swimming. If I kept still, I could see a little bit, but the minute I moved, I was blinded again. So I reclined and kept perfectly still. When Bobby called back to check on me I told him I was doing better, and was going to take a nap. Then I closed my eyes and didn't wake up again until after sundown.

With my eyes closed, I eased myself upright and sat on the side of the bed. When I opened my eyes, I could see. But when I stood, the room began circling around me. Very slowly and carefully, grabbing onto chairs and walls, I moved into the living room, eased back down in my chair beside the desk, and closed my eyes. When I opened them again, the light of a new morning was streaming into my apartment.

It took nearly a month for the headache, dizziness, and blurred vision to go away, but the important thing was that I was still alive. God had a plan for my life. The adventure was continuing.

One day a friend called to check on my condition. After I told him, he said, "You know, Harold, if you had more faith, you'd be rid of this cancer. I'd like to pray with you right now, and if you will just believe and have faith, you will be completely healed."

I was too mad to hear his words as he prayed. Was every Christian who had an illness, sat in a wheelchair, or lay in a hospital lacking faith? Was our health the only valid measure of our relationship with God? I couldn't accept that. God could heal me with a snap of His fingers, and if He wanted to do that I was more than ready. But wasn't it by faith that I'd surrendered myself to God's will as I lay on what I thought was my deathbed just a few days before?

Since God wants only what is best for us, why shouldn't I surrender to His plan, whatever it was? I thought of the Apostle Paul who asked God to remove a thorn in his flesh. But God said, "My grace is sufficient for you, for my power is made perfect in weakness" (2 Cor. 12:9). Though God was allowing me to suffer for awhile, I had to believe that because He loved me this trial would work for my ultimate good. I could place myself in the perfect will of God without reservation. Someday I might say with Paul, "For Christ's sake, I delight in weaknesses, in insults, in hardships, in persecutions, in difficulties. For when I am weak, then I am strong" (2 Cor. 12:10). I thought about how my biggest failure had become the real legacy of my life. I was a convict in prison, yet God used that experience for His glory. The significance of my life was not what I achieved, but what God chose to do through me in my weakness and failures. This was evidence of faith. Through prison, heartache, loneliness, pain, and illness, God was teaching me some tremendous lessons about faith and trust. I thought again of Job and how he was driven in desperation to a greater faith in God, despite his well-intentioned but empty-headed friends. God wanted to accomplish the same in me. Then I would rejoice with Peter who wrote that grief and trials "have come so that your faith—of greater worth than gold, which perishes even though refined by fire—may be proved genuine and may result in praise, glory and honor when Jesus Christ is revealed" (1 Peter 1:7). Unlike man, who sees good only in greatness, God was producing victory through defeat, and healing through brokenness. He was interested not so much in my successes, but in my faithfulness and obedience. After two months of treatment and a month to recuperate, I returned to Dr. Devonshire's office. My skin was burned from the radiation, and I looked like a cooked lobster. The doctor again rammed the tube up my nose, broke the membrane and searched my sinuses.

After what seemed an incredibly long time, but was actually only a few minutes, he pulled the instrument out and muttered, "I don't understand this." He made a notation on my chart and then said again, "I don't understand it. I see all the damage from the radiation—you've been absolutely fried—but there isn't a trace of cancer. As far as I can tell, all the cancer cells have burned up."

"Does that mean I'm healed?"

"It means you're clean as a whistle—for the time being."

"If I meet a pretty woman, can I get married?"

"No marriage, no relationships."

"Why not? You tell me I'm clean as a whistle."

"It can come back at any time," he said with a sigh. "An airline pilot had the same kind of cancer as you and asked if he should get married; he'd met a young flight attendant. I advised him not to, but he went ahead and married her anyway." He paused for emphasis. "His cancer came back, and he passed away just a few weeks ago, leaving his wife and their baby. That's why I don't think you should get attached to anyone."

"I suppose you want to check me again once in a while?"

"Every three months."

"Before I leave, I wonder if you would examine my throat. It's almost impossible for me to swallow."

Dr. Devonshire took a look and said, "It's too swollen for me to tell what's wrong. I'll prescribe some medication to deaden the pain. Come back next week and we'll take another look."

The medicine did reduce the pain, but only slightly. I still could barely swallow. When Dr. Devonshire looked at it again, the swelling had gone down. "This is the worst throat I've ever seen," he said. "It's almost completely closed by scar tissue." The only solution was to head to yet another doctor who, for the next twelve Mondays, put me under general anesthetic and rammed a tube down my throat, opening it so that I could eat some solid food.

The news that the cancer was gone was cause for celebration. Though the radiation burned away good cells—such as my saliva glands—with the bad cells, I didn't mind losing a few parts. "I had some extra parts to start with, anyway," I quipped to some concerned friends. "An eight cylinder car can run on six cylinders, and so can I." Of course, I'd have to learn how to coast down hills to save gas. I'd have to drive at a slower speed and not strain the engine. But the important thing was that my engine was still running. I was eager to get back to doing God's work.

But that wasn't so easy. I was still physically very weak. Because I had no saliva, I had to carry a glass or container of water with me wherever I went. When people saw me sneaking sips from the bottle I carried, they probably thought I was getting buzzed. But it was just water to keep my throat from turning to shoe leather.

I took one day to visit Michael Godwin. I had arranged for several members of the Atlanta Falcons to go into the prison to conduct a football clinic and play basketball with the inmates, and I promised Michael I'd try to come myself. We had talked almost every week by phone, and I'd faithfully sent him his

allowance. My support of Michael and several other prison inmates was the one aspect of my work that continued throughout
my illness. But it had been nearly six months since I'd been in
a prison.

When the group arrived, Michael introduced himself to everyone. I was wearing a wide-brimmed hat to protect my now sensitive face from the sun. Michael shook my hand, thanked me
for coming, and moved on without recognizing me. For the next
hour I stood and watched the program. Finally I said something
to Michael, and he stopped in his tracks and stared at me.

"It's you!" he said. He ran over to me. "I didn't recognize
you!" I could see tears welling up in his eyes. "Why didn't you
tell me you were so sick? You lied to me. You're dying!"

We moved over to a bench and sat down. It was true that I
hadn't told him all the details of my illness. I'd felt it was better
that way and didn't want him to worry. For the rest of the afternoon, he wouldn't leave my side. Finally he blurted out the
thought plaguing his mind. "What will I do if you die?"

"Michael, if I don't make it, you're taken care of. In fact,
you'd be better off if I die. I've made arrangements with Edwin
Tucker, the chairman of my board, and he's promised to continue
fighting for your freedom. I've got a life insurance policy, so the
money will be there to educate you. You'll have far more if I
die than if I live. So you'd better hope I die."

"That's not funny. You mean the world to me. I wouldn't be
alive if it weren't for you."

"Michael, I love you like a son. I really don't think I'm going
to die right now. God has me here for a purpose, and the doctors
believe they've destroyed all the cancer, at least for now. But I
want to assure you that you're taken care of if anything does
happen. Don't you worry. Just stay on course and don't lose sight
of your goals. Keep on studying and doing what God's called
you to do and one day you're going to be free."

The problem with my throat persisted despite the weekly tub-
ings. Within twenty-four hours, the passageway, left to itself,
would nearly close, making it almost impossible for me to
swallow. The situation required daily attention, and one day the

doctor said he had no choice but to remove my vocal cords and insert an eating tube below my voice box. I wouldn't be able to talk, and if I had a craving for a hamburger and fries, I'd have to tear them into little pieces and cram them down the tube without tasting a thing.

"Can you imagine me telling my girlfriend, 'Hey, kiss my tube?' " I asked the doctor.

"Harold, you're crazy," was all he could manage.

"I won't let you do that," I said. "That's no way for a person to live."

"Then your only other alternative is to do for yourself what I do when you're under general anesthetic," he said.

"What does that involve?"

"Well," he began, "all you've got to do is shove a two-and-a-half-foot long rubber rod down your throat."

"Is that all?" I said sarcastically.

"Every day for the rest of your life."

"Unless God chooses to heal me," I said.

It took half a day the first time I tried it on my own. There was blood, vomit and tears all over the bathroom before it was accomplished. The second day was only slightly better. I wanted to quit, except I kept thinking of the alternative. At least this way I'd have a life. So every morning, I'd face the mirror with my feet spread wide and my head tilted back as far as possible. Then I'd thread that inch-thick rubber rod down my esophagus all the way to my stomach. Then I'd pull it out and repeat the procedure.

Sometimes, my throat was so constricted that the tube would snag and bend on a ridge of scar tissue. That produced bleeding and soreness for days. In the misery of that experience, one thing kept me going: the thought that God had provided a way for me to live and speak. As the doctor said, all I had to do was shove a two-and-a-half-foot rubber rod down my throat. Gradually, over a number of weeks, there were fewer problems and I was able to complete the procedure in a matter of seconds.

It is amazing what a brush with death will do for one's perspective. I had noticed after leaving prison, that I appreciated the small things in life much more than before. For example, in prison

I longed for clean sheets; afterwards I gladly thanked God for them every day. Now I noticed my appreciation for small things growing stronger. I found special joy in talking on the telephone and telling someone, "I love you." It was a pleasure driving to the store for an ice cream cone, seeing the beauty of a tree, or enjoying a good laugh with a friend. I didn't realize how precious my taste buds were until I couldn't taste. I thanked God for them as they began to return, and I could again taste and smell. I didn't know how wonderful my eyes were until I blacked out and wondered if I would ever see again. I thanked God daily for the sights He allowed me to view.

Most of all, I thanked God for my voice. At first thought, it seemed impossible that I could be grateful for my rubber tube. But when I realized that it enabled me to speak, swallow, eat, and lead a fairly normal life, I gladly thanked Him. There were additional benefits. The tube was very humbling. It kept my feet on the ground, and enabled me to relate with hurting people. It was a daily reminder of how healthy I was, how blessed I was to be able to walk, see sunsets, breath the sea air, and feel love. I would take that all for granted were it not for my tube. Today, I wouldn't trade it for anything in the world.

Another area for thanksgiving was a blossoming friendship with Bill Curry, at the time head football coach at Georgia Tech, and later named head coach at the University of Alabama. Georgia Tech was just fifteen minutes from my home, and as my strength increased Bill often invited me to lunch and football practice. I spoke several times to his team and joined them on the sidelines during home games. Bill frequently called just to check my condition, or dropped me a note saying, "Me fight with Big Harold." That was in reference to a story I'd told his team about Frito, the Puerto Rican inmate who had stood with me against a gang of black toughs and announced, "Me stand with Big Harold." His courage had averted a fight that would surely have left me a bloody mess.

Another special friend was Dan Reeves, head coach of the Denver Broncos. Randy Gradishar and Coach Reeves invited me to come out to Denver for a week. I flew with the team to Seattle and stood on the sidelines as they defeated the Seahawks for the division championship.

Dr. James Dobson and the staff of Focus on the Family were a third source of encouragement. In late November, Dr. Dobson invited me to California and we taped two radio programs. This was the first trip I'd taken since my operation in April. His broadcasts allowed me to talk to more people than I'd addressed in all of my previous speaking engagements combined. While I was in California, Dr. Dobson also encouraged my work on my first book, *Twice Pardoned*.

At the end of the year, I again endured the awful threading of Dr. Devonshire's tube through my head. The verdict remained, "No cancer." He gave me permission to resume speaking at a limited pace of one appearance a week. I began slowly, addressing a couple of churches that supported my work financially.

One evening I spoke at a church in Atlanta. I gave my testimony to the congregation, telling them about how God rescued me from prison and my bout with cancer. After my talk, an elderly woman was among the many who came forward to greet me. Her face glowed as she grabbed my hand. "Young man, God must love you very much," she said. "What a joy it is to be chosen by God to suffer for Him."

The look on this woman's face told me she understood suffering. Her faith was tough. I thought often about her words. She was right. It was a joy—just the opposite of what most people think—to suffer for Christ.

There were other opportunities to speak to several professional sports teams. But with so many invitations available, by the middle of 1985 I was struggling to keep my schedule under control. The appearances on Focus on the Family opened new opportunities all over the country. One week I spoke twenty-one times in sixteen high schools. That wasn't the kind of schedule my doctor had in mind. But each time I returned to Dr. Devonshire, he found no trace of cancer.

Meanwhile, Focus on the Family published my book, *Twice Pardoned*, and began developing two films by the same title. Shortly after the release of my book, I walked into a Christian bookstore in Atlanta. During a conversation with the couple that owned the store, the woman said, "There's a young woman who comes in here, and her story is a lot like yours. She went to the same cancer center you did, but her cancer has come back and she's very depressed. She struggles with bitterness toward God."

"I understand the feeling," I said. "Tell me more about her."

"Well, she says she's seen you before. She came in, picked up your book and said, 'I've seen that man before.'"

"What does she do?"

"Said she was a flight attendant."

Suddenly I remembered the girl I'd met in St. Joseph's waiting room one day. "Wait a minute. How old is she?"

"About thirty."

"Linda somebody?"

"Linda O'Malley."

Linda was living in the apartment complex behind the bookstore. The couple gave me her phone number, and I left a message on her answering machine, reintroducing myself. "I'd love to talk to you," I said. "Please call; it's important."

Linda called back and agreed, after some hesitancy, to let me take her to lunch. I was excited about our date, remembering how I was struck by her beauty the first time we met. When Linda opened the door, my anticipation turned to shock. She was so thin, and had a scar like mine on the left side of her neck. Her hair was short, and she wore a sleeveless dress that hung on her bony frame like a pup tent. Her left shoulder was dark, like a badly-cooked steak.

Noticing my stares, she said, "I've started radiation again. The cancer came back to my shoulder. The dark spot is where they accidentally burned me with radiation."

As we ate lunch, we compared our experiences. We'd had the exact same cancer and treatment. We'd each had lymph nodes removed, and each of us had our saliva glands burned away. Like me, Linda carried a glass of water wherever she went. The only difference was that her cancer had returned; mine remained in remission.

"Oh, there's one other difference," I said.

"And what's that?"

"My scar is prettier than yours!" Linda tried to smile, but it had been so long since she'd laughed that the smile looked awkward. Then I got serious. "I'm told you're struggling in your relationship with Christ."

She nodded and quietly said, "I've questioned why God would allow the cancer to come back. I don't have any answers, but I'm holding onto Him. He's all I have."

We talked for a long time and I was amazed how open we were, considering how little we knew each other. For the first time, I found myself telling someone my deepest fears, anxieties and gripes, because I knew Linda understood. "The radiologist never told me what to expect," I said. "He just told me the radiation would destroy my teeth, but I've yet to lose one."

Linda nodded knowingly.

"It bothered me that some of the nurses seemed so calloused," she said. "I had trouble sleeping, and one morning a nurse woke me up at four o'clock just to weigh me. Another told me, 'If the cancer doesn't kill you, the chemotherapy will.'"

I told Linda about my throat problems, and how for weeks no one seemed willing to take my complaint seriously. Linda shook her head as my recitation brought back memories for her. "I started spitting up blood last August," she said. "The doctor X-rayed me and found they'd fried the top of one of my lungs. They were treating my shoulder, but went too low with the radiation."

I looked at her and felt intense empathy. Having suffered as much as she had, it was tragic that she should endure further pain because of a technician's error.

As I drove Linda back to her apartment after lunch, I asked about her future plans. She sighed heavily. "It's been two-and-a-half years since I've worked," she said. "I don't know what I'm going to do. I'll probably lose my apartment; my money's all gone."

I realized Linda needed more than just words of reassurance. God had given me an understanding for her, and He had also recently blessed me with financial resources. "Linda, don't worry about losing your apartment," I said. "I'll be over tomorrow to pay the rent."

During the next few weeks, we went out to eat frequently. She told me about how she was taking a sewing class and thought she could accept small sewing jobs to earn a little income, as soon as she could afford a sewing machine. The next day, I bought her a deluxe sewing machine that she had picked out. "You go ahead and sew," I told her. "It will be good therapy." For the first time since we met, I saw her smile. The glow in her face was all the thanks I needed. I was just grateful that God allowed me to help her.

Our favorite restaurant was a little place Linda found called "Eat Those Vegetables." That became her frequent exhortation to me as I reverted to my old pattern of gorging myself. I quickly put on weight, but she encouraged me in a kind way to let the air out of my "spare tire" by improving my eating habits.

This restaurant had outstanding vegetable dishes, and we'd sit for hours, eating, drinking our water, and talking. "This is a five-glass conversation," I joked to her one day. She quickly pointed out that she'd had more water than me, and we laughed to think we sounded like two kids vying for the upper hand.

One of the hardest aspects of our illness was losing people whom we had considered close friends. Linda told me how she and her boyfriend had talked of marriage before she had cancer. "He dropped me as soon as I got sick. Another guy was afraid our kids would be born with the disease, so he bailed out."

"The same thing happened to me," I said. "I haven't told anyone about it, but I was dating a woman, and we'd talked about marriage. But then I got sick, and she changed. She actually asked whether my cancer was contagious, and if I'd be able to father children. It was as if I'd become a leper to her."

The more we talked, the better I felt. Just discussing our shared experiences and feelings was extremely therapeutic. "You're helping me understand myself better," I told her.

It was encouraging to see Linda gradually regain her strength over the months. Color returned to her face, and she put on some weight. Before long, she began thinking she was healed. She talked about some long-range goals—to return to college and perhaps go to the mission field. In the meantime, she decided to return to work with the airline.

In November of 1986, shortly before I left to start filming for "Twice Pardoned," Linda called. She was just weeks away from going back to work with the airline. I expected her to sound excited. But her voice was hesitant, and I got a sinking feeling in my stomach.

There was silence at the other end of the line, and I thought she was crying. "Linda, are you okay?"

"Harold, I need you," she said.

"What's wrong?"

"The doctor wants me to go to Chicago for some special tests."

"Oh, Linda. I'm sorry."

"I don't have money for the plane ticket."

"I'll cover the ticket on one condition: that you call me as soon as you return. I want a full report."

A week later, she called. "The cancer has spread to my pelvis," she said. She didn't need to say any more. We both knew what that meant. Within a short period of time, her doctor discovered the tumor had spread to the stem of her brain and was growing bigger. It caused her double vision and incredible headaches, but the doctors told her they couldn't operate and that additional radiation therapy would kill her. The only possibility, they said, was chemotherapy. But it would only provide temporary relief, and would cause such intense sickness that she'd wish she was dead.

One night she called to ask my advice, but as gently as possible I told her that a decision about continuing a temporary treatment was one that only she could make. A few days later she called back to say she would decline the chemotherapy, because it would just postpone the inevitable. She then announced that she was going to fly home to Colorado to be with her parents. "They need me," she said quietly.

It was painful to realize how attached I'd grown to this godly woman. I didn't want to lose Linda, yet I knew that any day could be her last. That only reminded me of my own mortality.

I had to constantly remember that tomorrow, my cancer could also return.

I suppose it would be normal to want to retreat from a relationship like the one I had with Linda. Why should I open myself to more pain and suffering? Why should I love her if I'd only lose her? But that wasn't God's perspective. As He said through Paul, we are to "comfort those in any trouble with the comfort we ourselves have received from God" (2 Cor. 1:4). No matter how painful, I had to reach out and help hurting people, just as so many friends had reached out to me when I was ill. I determined that as long as God allowed me to live, I would love the Lindas God brought into my life.

Chapter Eleven

CRYSTAL AND MARY SUE

Following my first broadcasts on Focus on the Family, I received an avalanche of mail. Then Dr. Dobson made an announcement about my illness, asking people to pray for me. That produced additional letters full of get well wishes and encouragement. Unfortunately, I was too sick to even read, much less answer, the majority of them.

One day when I was feeling more energetic than usual, I sorted through a pile of mail. My eye caught a pink envelope from a young woman in New Jersey. Inside was a warm and cordial message written in clear script on flowery stationery. The writer said she shared my burden for young people, and that the radio program had made a big impact on her life. "You've suffered more than anybody I know," she wrote. "You were in prison on false charges for ten years, and now you are fighting for your life from cancer. I don't know what the future will bring, but I want you to know that I am praying for you. Harold Morris, you are my hero." It was signed, Crystal Lavelle.

I sensed that this woman, whoever she was, really cared, and in appreciation I managed to jot her a brief note of thanks. A few weeks later I received another encouraging letter from her, and again I sent a brief note in return. After several more letters, she wrote, "If you send me your picture, I'll send you mine."

I followed up on the request, and waited expectantly for

Crystal's next envelope. When it arrived the following week, my heart raced with expectation. I knew nothing about her other than what I'd gleaned from her letters. She lived in New Jersey. She was twenty-eight years old. She loved young people. She prayed for me daily. Her relationship with the Lord was the most important thing in her life. I did my best to read between the lines, and in my mind I pictured her as having long blond hair and blue eyes.

I held my breath as I slit open the envelope. Slowly I pulled out the picture. I took one look, and instantly my eyes welled up with tears. I held the picture in front of me, and cried as hard as I've ever cried. Crystal Lavelle was nothing like I'd envisioned. She didn't have blond hair and blue eyes. She was not a full-grown woman with an all-American figure. She was sitting in a wheelchair, her body twisted by cerebral palsy.

In an accompanying note, Crystal explained that she had been born with the disease, and had spent virtually all of her life in institutions. "My parents gave me up at birth," she wrote matter-of-factly.

I stared at her face, which bore the most joyful expression I'd ever seen. Her mouth was crooked, but her teeth gleamed. She seemed to be laughing through a smile that beamed from ear to ear. All I could think about were the lines from her first letter. She said I'd suffered more than anybody she'd ever known. She said I was her hero. But compared to her, I had never suffered.

As soon as I regained some composure, I wrote a note to her: "Please call me collect as soon as you get this letter."

Two days later, I was sitting in my living room contemplating my future. I had completed the radiation treatments and was trying to recover before my visit to Dr. Devonshire. I wondered if the cancer was gone. I wondered if I could ever speak again. I was practically broke, and increasingly concerned about finding a way to earn some money. Suddenly, the phone rang, and the operator asked if I would accept a collect call from Crystal Lavelle. I authorized the reversal of charges.

"Harol'? Harol', is that 'ou?" she shouted, her voice was

fragile, but loud. I battled my emotions as I listened to her struggling to enunciate each word.

"Yes, it's me," I said. I thanked her for calling, and told her how much her letters meant to me.

"Thank 'ou!" she practically squealed. "I pray for 'ou every day!" She asked me about Dr. Dobson, and said she also prayed for him and Focus on the Family every day. Her voice was so cheerful, so positive. I had to learn more about her, but it was hard because she wanted to ask all the questions and her voice was difficult to understand.

Finally, I managed to tell her, "Crystal, you don't know how hard I cried when I saw your photo. Compared to you, I don't know what suffering is. You make me feel as if I've never been sick a day in my life. My prison was nothing compared to yours."

We continued writing on a regular basis, she with the help of an attendant named Donna, which explained the beautiful handwriting. We also talked often to each other by phone. Whenever I called, the attendant on duty would set the phone down and go find Crystal. Then I would hear, far off in the distant halls of the home, a guttural scream of excitement. "Harol'!" she would yell, not quite able to mouth the final consonant. "Harol'!" I pictured her racing through the halls in her electric wheelchair, trying to reach the phone as fast as possible.

Our phone calls, I knew, were one of the highlights of her week. She talked with exclamation marks in her voice. The first thing she generally said was that she'd been praying for me. The last thing she said before we hung up was that she loved me. And in between, our conversation centered around the Lord.

It took awhile to piece together her life story. "How long have you been a Christian?" I asked her one evening.

"Three years!"

"And how did you come to know the Lord?"

"I was 'wenty-five year' old. I wanted to commit suicide. But I prayed, and God 'aved me!"

It was so simple, so obvious to her. "Crystal, do you go to church?"

"Sure I do!"

"Do you read your Bible?"

She gave a lovely laugh and then said, "I 'isten to Focus on the Family every morning. And I 'isten to tapes. And the pastor's wife visit' me every week!"

It dawned on me that perhaps Crystal couldn't read. But she was obviously growing in the Lord. She was getting fed.

"Harol'! I've written some song' for Jesuh! Would 'ou 'ike to hear them?"

"I'd like nothing more."

A few days later I received a cassette. As I played it, I cried again as she sang, "Jesuh, I 'ove 'ou. I 'ove 'ou with all my 'eart. Jesuh, I 'ove 'ou. I give 'ou my all!"

I'd noticed that when she got very excited, it was hard to understand her. And as she sang, I tried to imagine how she strained her mouth, and stretched her neck and body trying to express the love she felt so deeply in her heart. This woman knew what it meant to love the Lord.

I didn't know what her financial situation was, but since she was institutionalized, I figured she could probably use some help. So I mailed her some money. She immediately called me, telling me not to send any more.

"Crystal, I want to give it to you. You can do anything you want with it. It's yours."

"No, I can't take it!" she protested.

"Isn't there anything you'd like to buy?" I asked her.

She was quiet for a moment. "It's not right for me to take it."

"Crystal, I prayed about it and believe God wanted me to send it to you. Are you going to rob me of that blessing?"

She paused again before saying, "I will pray about it."

The next time we talked, she said she would accept my gifts on one condition: "'ou have to let me send 'ou gifts."

"Honey, the money is yours to do with as you want," I said with a chuckle.

"I will also tithe to my church," she announced.

Shortly thereafter, I received a small package in the mail. It contained a painting she'd done on a six-by-eight-inch piece of cardboard. The picture consisted of hundreds of lines of bright red, orange, yellow, green, and blue paint, and in the far right corner were her initials, CL. I don't know much about art, but I keep the painting on my desk, and look at it every day. To me it's more valuable than a Picasso, and I wouldn't trade it for any price.

As I got to know Crystal better, I learned she had endured two operations that totally fused the vertebrae in her back, and she'd spent a year immobilized inside a body cast. Meanwhile, her parents had become wealthy through business. She told me that for years she was bitter toward them for having abandoned her in an institution, and that the bitterness grew to hatred by the time she was twenty-five. She also hated the world for giving up on her, for not loving her.

The hatred finally grew so intense, she knew she had to do something. So she did the only thing she could think of. She rolled her wheelchair into a dark corner of her room, and cried out to God for help, asking Him to remove the bitterness. He did, replacing it with a new love and understanding for her parents. Along with that love, He gave her a new reason to live— that is, to see her parents one day meet her Lord Jesus Christ.

Toward that goal, Crystal spent six hours every day at "workshop." That was her job, and during those six hours she screwed nuts and bolts together. It was hard work for Crystal, and she was paid by the piece. All year she saved her nickels and dimes, pooling the money she earned to buy a plane ticket to visit her parents in California. For her, the trips were well worth it—just to tell them she loved them—and that Jesus did, too.

I talked to her after she returned from one of those trips, and asked how it went. "It was okay," she said, without her typical enthusiasm.

"Did you do anything fun together?"

"We went shopping. But Harol', I couldn't wait to get back home to my friends. My parents don't understand me."

"I can imagine that you're a painful reminder to them," I said.

"Harol', please pray for them." I could hear tears in her voice. "My parents don't know Jesuh, and they're getting older."

One day she told me that my love for families and young people touched her so deeply that she arranged to be transported to a nearby high school where she spoke to the entire student body about how I'd landed in prison because I hung around with the wrong crowd. She urged them to pick their friends carefully, and to avoid drugs and immoral sex. Then she told them how Jesus had transformed both of our lives, and how even in our own prisons of a wheelchair and a state penitentiary, we were more free than most people.

"Harol', they gave me a standing ovation!" she said excitedly. "And they've asked me to come back and speak again!"

I was stunned. Here was a person with incredible physical limitations going out and speaking to kids. I couldn't help thinking of all the excuses I'd heard from Christians about why they didn't witness. But Crystal didn't know any excuses. She was an inspiration. She was proof that there is no limitation for a person who wants to be used by God.

For two-and-a-half years, Crystal and I carried on our long-distance correspondence and conversations. She was always there to encourage me when I felt down, to offer a kind word of hope, to ask me about my most recent speaking tour and how the audiences had responded, to tell me she loved me. Then one day she shared with me something very private. Harol', there's one thing I want that only 'ou can give."

"Crystal, there's nothing I would deny you. You've given me far more than I can ever give back."

"Harol', before I die I want 'ou to come spend a day with me in New Jersey.

"I promise you I'll come, and you'll be my date! We'll go to the park, and I'll take you shopping at the mall."

"Would you really do that, Harol'?"

"Crystal, I promise you I will. Not only that, but I'm going to push you, and I'll grease up the wheels so they won't squeak. We're going to have ourselves some kind of fun!"

In the spring of 1987, I finally had the opportunity to fulfill my pledge. Accompanied by Rick Christian from Focus on the Family, I flew to New Jersey, rented a car, and drove to the institution. We arrived two hours earlier than expected, but she'd been ready since the crack of dawn. When told she had visitors, I heard her top-of-the-lungs scream from the back of the home. "Harol'! Harol'!" She came rolling around the corner in her motorized wheelchair, her face lit with a thousand-watt smile. "Harol'!" she beamed.

I bent over, put my arms around Crystal's little twisted body, and for a long time we just sat there holding each other and crying. Finally I stepped back to get a good look at her. She was wearing her best satin dress, with a matching cream-colored ribbon braided through her hair. Around her neck was a beautiful gold crucifix hanging on a gold chain. And in her ears were diamond earrings. "My you are a beautiful woman," I said, and never had those words carried more meaning.

It was a vacation day for Crystal, so she didn't have to go to "workshop." We sat in the front room of the home and for two hours reminisced about our two-and-a-half years of letters and phone calls, and what the Lord was doing in our lives.

"Harol', I pray for 'ou every day," she said.

"I know, Crystal. And God honors those prayers."

"Every day after lunch, I have one hour to pray. It's hard sometimes to keep that up because of other things I do, but it's the most important hour of my day."

There were several other residents in the room, and I noticed many were in pretty bad shape. Several of them eased their wheelchairs close to where we talked. One boy in particular kept looking at Crystal with a twisted grin on his face. I found out his name was Ralph, and later I asked Crystal about him.

"Ralph's all right," she answered. "He used to be my boyfriend!"

One of the other residents heard that and added, "Ralph flirts with all the girls. He's got another girl now."

I shook my head in amazement. Even in this little world of twisted bodies and unimaginable affliction, there was a need for courtship.

Crystal asked if I'd noticed her earrings. I nodded. "Are they real diamonds?"

"They sure are! I bought them with the money 'ou gave me."

"They're beautiful."

"I like nice things!" she beamed. "Harol', I thank 'ou for the money."

"Crystal, it's a joy to send it to you."

"'ou know something? You always send the right amount. I know God's in it because 'ou always send just what I need. Always!"

At that moment, I felt a great satisfaction. How wonderful to know that Crystal could buy nice things, and not worry about whether she could afford them. She had also asked me to send her two cases of my books. She gave them to everyone who visited the home, and sold them to people at her church. It was her own little ministry, and she donated her proceeds to Focus on the Family.

As we talked, a large black woman with graying hair walked over and sat on the edge of an armchair. Crystal introduced her as Mary Sue, who was in charge of the kitchen.

"Me and Crystal, we go back a long time," Mary Sue said, fingering a curl in Crystal's hair. They looked at each other and smiled. In that glance was more love than I'd ever seen displayed in all my life.

Most people would not have given Mary Sue a second look. Her clothes were worn, and a lifetime of service was displayed in her tired feet. She was wearing a pair of inexpensive vinyl sandals that exposed a collection of bunions and calluses that covered her toes. Her feet themselves were broad and worn, and on them you could see the miles. And when she walked, she shuffled slowly. I knew every step was taken in pain.

I asked Mary Sue to tell me about her life. She said she was one of fifteen children, and had lost her mother when she was young. So Mary Sue became the mother to seven of her younger brothers and sisters. Then came a bad marriage, the birth of a handicapped son, and a continuing life of nonstop work and sleepless nights. She supported her family and extended relatives by doing the same thing she did at home—caring for people. She'd served Crystal for twenty years, becoming the mother that

Crystal never had, loving her day by day as she grew from a small child to an adult of thirty.

Mary Sue said she arrived at the institution early each morning and worked all day, preparing breakfast, lunch, and dinner for the fifteen handicapped residents, plus staff. Then in the evening, she returned home to prepare dinner for her grandchildren and her severely handicapped son—a son whom she'd been loving and serving for forty years. I knew it was love that drove Mary Sue. She didn't do all this work for money, because there wasn't much financial payoff.

"Mary Sue, it would mean a great deal if you did not have to cook lunch today," I said. "I want lunch to be my treat. I'll go out and buy food for the entire home and all of the workers."

"No, no, Mr. Morris. You will be *our* guest."

"Mary Sue, I insist. I want to buy lunch for everybody, to give you a break, and to—"

"No, I—"

I turned to Crystal. "What's your favorite food in the whole world?"

"Mr. Morris—" Mary Sue began again.

"Crystal, your favorite food?"

Crystal leaned her head back to her shoulders and burst out laughing. "Chinese! Chinese! Chinese!" she chortled.

"Can the other residents eat Chinese food?" I asked Mary Sue. She nodded reluctantly.

"Then we'll be back in a half hour with enough food for an army. Is there anything else you want, Crystal?"

She leaned her head back again and laughed with excitement. "Milkshake! Milkshake!"

Rick and I returned with a huge cardboard box filled with just about everything on the Chinese restaurant's menu. Waiting in the dining room, surrounding a sprawling formica table were Crystal and most of the other residents. They were in wheelchairs, and all were severely disabled.

Crystal's right hand was completely useless, and she could only move the two small fingers of her left hand. A fork was placed between those fingers so that she could eat. I couldn't help noticing that her feet, which had never taken a single step, were wrapped in thick shocks of wool.

I looked at some of the others eating with her. Susan not only had cerebral palsy, but she was also blind. Her food was mixed in a large bowl, and an attendant put a fork in her hand and then moved the hand to the bowl. Brian looked to be about twenty-five, and had a Stephen King paperback beside him. He wore a pair of binoculars around his neck. As he ate, he took short breaks to watch birds outside the window. Terry was in her sixties and talked a mile a minute during the entire meal. But I didn't understand a word she said. Joseph had a small body like Crystal, but his head was oversized. He told me he listened to the "Focus on the Family" radio program with Crystal every morning, and that he'd read my book. Little Mary, with a urinary drainage bag strapped beside her on the wheelchair, wore most of her food on her blouse before lunch was over. It was a circus of excitement, presided over by Mary Sue.

After the meal, I obtained clearance to take Crystal shopping at the mall. But there was one contingency. Even though I had help from Rick Christian, an attendant from the home also had to accompany us. Mary Sue agreed to go along, providing she was back in time to prepare dinner. I carried Crystal to the car, my hand braced against her knotted back. I gently set her in the seat, and fastened a belt around her waist. After loading her wheelchair in the trunk, the four of us set off for the mall on what was a postcard-perfect afternoon.

We started in one of the large department stores. "Pick any dress you want," I told Crystal, as I wheeled her through racks of the women's clothing department. She giggled and rolled her head as we scavenged about for a petite size six. Dozens of dresses were held out for her, and dismissed with a shake of her head and a few summary words: "Too blue." "Wrong neckline." "Not soft enough." "No thanks."

Then Mary Sue held up a shimmering sky blue dress, the bodice of which was covered with little spangles that glinted in the light. It was the type of dress a young woman might wear to a senior prom. Crystal rolled her head, and screamed with excitement. Other shoppers turned and stared. "She likes it," I said.

"I'll buy you another," I told her, and she screamed again. We found her a cotton-candy soft pink dress that had Crystal's name and Sunday morning written all over it. She would wear it to church.

As we headed for the cash register, I followed behind Mary Sue. I thought about how she'd stood faithfully by Crystal and probably hadn't bought anything for herself in years.

"We forgot something," I said. Mary Sue turned around. "I want you to pick out a dress, too."

She looked at me like I was crazy. "No, Mr. Morris. I couldn't."

"You find yourself something pretty, Mary Sue."

"I wouldn't think of doing such a thing, Mr. Morris. You've already been so good to us all."

"Either you can pick it out, or I'll pick it for you. And if I pick it, I can guarantee you'll be sorry." I draped my arm around her shoulder and gently nudged her back toward the racks.

Within ten minutes, she was trying to decide between two gorgeous dresses, both size twenty-two-and-a-half. She asked Crystal which one she liked the best.

I shook my head. "They're both yours," I said, taking the dresses from her and heading for the cash register.

Five other women stood in line before me. When my turn came, the clerk took the four dresses and gave me a funny look. "It was hard to find something my size," I said, placing my hand on my hip. "But if I lose a few icky pounds, I think I can squeeze into them. Of course, they're not exactly my color. I'd wanted something more lavender."

The clerk rang up the purchase as fast as she could, without looking up, and the four of us laughed all the way out the store.

Again I was walking behind Mary Sue. Her calloused feet looked like they hurt, and I knew she probably didn't have a comfortable pair of dress shoes in her closet. I also knew she couldn't afford to buy a pair for herself. "One more stop," I said. "Mary Sue, let's find you a nice pair of shoes to go with your dresses. And a purse to match." She stopped dead in her tracks and turned around in shock. "Don't even bother protesting," I said. "It's something I want to do for you." "But Mr. Morris—" "Mary Sue, there's a store up ahead." We stopped there and at two other stores, but nobody carried her size. Her feet were too broad, and wouldn't fit into the narrow confines of a pair of pumps. We were running out of time, but there was one other shoe store in the mall. I waited several feet away as she approached the clerk, and inquired if the store had her special size. As she talked, the woman looked her up and down, and then glanced at another customer and rolled her eyes. Mary Sue was not the typical customer. She had no purse and no pockets, which in the woman's mind probably meant no money. Her clothes were wrinkled; her hair unkept. She was black, and all of the other customers in the store were white.

"I'll be with you in a minute," the woman said, and proceeded to help everybody else in the store first. We waited patiently until the store was empty. Finally the clerk turned back to Mary Sue, scowled down at her feet, and then disappeared into the back room to check for her size. She returned a minute later with one box.

"It's all we have in your size," she said. "One pair of off-white pumps."

"That's what I need," Mary Sue said, easing herself slowly into one of the narrow chairs. The woman stood opposite her, again looking down at her feet.

"Do you have a pair of stockings or hosiery?" she asked.

Mary Sue shook her head.

"You'll need something on your feet before you try these on."

I watched from distance, prepared to offer her the socks off my feet if the woman didn't come up with something herself. The clerk disappeared again into a back room and returned with two plastic trash bags, which she held out to Mary Sue.

"For your feet," she said gruffly.

Mary Sue shook the bags out and, without complaining, slipped them over her feet. The woman handed her one of the shoes. Mary Sue squeezed one foot in, and then held her hand out for the other. Mary Sue put it on and stood up. She looked pitiful walking around in the trash bags and fancy shoes, and my heart broke knowing the humiliation I'd have felt if I was in her place. But if she was feeling anything, the only emotion that showed on her face was pure joy. The shoes fit, and her face beamed.

After purchasing the shoes and a purse to match, we finally headed for the car. No doubt about it, I was accompanied by two of the happiest women on earth. I also felt I was in the company of two of the holiest women as well.

Crystal had arranged for me to speak in her church that night. I was tired, my throat was sore, and I didn't feel like going. But I had promised Crystal I'd speak on one basis: that she introduce me. I didn't know quite what to expect, because I'd never before been to a church service on a Friday night. It was the end of the week, and people would be tired. They'd drag home for work, eat and land in front of the television. Or they'd grab some dinner and catch a movie. Maybe they'd read a good book, or flip through a magazine.

I expected thirty or forty people, but when we pulled up at the church, the parking lot was packed. A couple of hundred people were inside, warming up with the help of three musicians playing piano, bass guitar, and drums. Before long, a bongo player joined in, and the church was rocking with music.

When I pushed Crystal through the door, she was immediately surrounded by church members. People stopped their conversations and walked over to hug her. Others gave her little chicken-peck kisses on the cheek. One little girl had drawn a crayon picture on construction paper, and gave that to her. Another little boy had made a ring for her out of aluminum foil. I knew instantly that this was a church that loved people. Though I was a thousand miles away from home, I felt surrounded by family.

When the service started at eight o'clock, Crystal was sitting in her wheelchair in the front row. The first few minutes were devoted to singing of praise and worship, which Crystal belted out at the top of her lungs. Looking at the joy on her face, I realized how important praise was to her. She couldn't read the

Bible or comprehend complex sermon outlines. Her outlet for worship was in singing and making a joyful noise to the Lord.

After a brief welcome, the pastor turned the microphone over to Crystal to introduce me. She rolled her head back and in a little sweet voice that you had to struggle to understand, she simply said: "I want to introduce 'ou to my friend Harol'. I know he loves Jesuh, and I know he loves me. Please listen to what he has to say."

I had tears in my eyes when I stepped up to speak, and I found it difficult to think about anything other than the day I'd just spent with two incredible women. So I did something unusual. I scrapped my planned talk and spoke instead about what I considered to be the second most meaningful day of my life, second only to the day I became a Christian.

"That day happens to be today," I said. My message was a living illustration of faith and commitment—the faith of a young handicapped woman who supported an old ex-con through a serious illness, who prayed an hour a day, and who worked all year just to buy a ticket to visit the very people who abandoned her to an institution as a child; and the commitment of an aging black lady who raised seven of her brothers and sisters, who supported an extended family when her husband deserted her, and who worked all day in a hot kitchen to make life a little easier and a lot brighter for fifteen handicapped people.

"Today I saw more love displayed than I've ever seen before in my life," I said in closing. "It's the love of Christ, lived out in very ordinary everyday ways by two individuals whom most people would dismiss with hardly a glance. I know there is a special corner in heaven waiting for them . . . and for those among us who would follow Christ by following their example."

After I finished speaking, there wasn't a dry eye in the church. When the pastor gave an invitation, asking people to come forward who wanted to again renew their faith and commitment to each other, their families, and to Jesus Christ, the entire congregation crowded forward.

It was well past midnight when the doors of the church were shut. When I finally crawled into bed, I could think of no better way to have spent the night. I lay awake for a long time, thinking, remembering, and praying. As I finally drifted off to sleep, I thought about how one day I wanted to be greeted in heaven not by an angel, a choir, or a preacher wearing a clerical robe, but by a young woman in a blue-spangled dress, her body no longer twisted by the ravages of cerebral palsy. And right beside her would be a big-hearted black woman standing tall in a brand new dress and a pair of off-white pumps.

I continued to talk to Crystal frequently on the phone, and she constantly encouraged me in my faith. She didn't even realize how many people she was touching. One afternoon I called her from my motel before I was to speak to a large rally of some three thousand teenagers. "Crystal, will you pray for me tonight?" I asked after I told her about the crusade.

"Of course!"

"I'm going to tell them about you tonight, Crystal. Is there anything you want me to say?"

"Harol', tell them to stay out of trouble. Tell them to 'isten to 'ou. Tell them to 'isten to their parents. And tell them to trust Jesuh."

"I will tell them," I promised.

That night as I brought my message to a close, I talked about peer pressure and the importance of following positive role models. And then I told them about one of my heroes, Crystal Lavelle. As I finished my story, I said, "Young people, I talked to Crystal tonight, just before I came here. I asked her if there was anything she'd like to say. Can I tell you what she said?"

Perhaps it was my imagination, but it seemed like each of the kids leaned forward to catch the special words. After I repeated her message, I challenged them: "Are you going to do that? I'm going to ask you to come forward now and commit your lives to Christ."

For the next forty-five minutes, I and many counselors were inundated with young people. It was a powerful evening, because of a thirty-year-old woman imprisoned in a twisted body who had tough faith.

I'd heard some Christians say that if she really had faith she'd be healed—she'd jump out of that wheelchair and walk. What they didn't realize was that faith was what kept her in that wheelchair day after day, year after year, with enough love for God to speak to an entire student body about Jesus, enough love to fly to California to tell her parents about Jesus, and enough love to pray daily for a friend who was told he would die of cancer. That's faith!

One night Crystal called me about eleven o'clock, which was unusual because she was normally in bed by nine. She told me she'd been out to a special church function and had just arrived home. But she wasn't the same cheerful person I usually talked to. "Crystal, is something wrong?" I asked.

"Harol', I want you to pray for me. I'm not doing well physically."

In the years since I'd first known her, Crystal had never complained about her condition. I knew she had to be hurting bad to say even this. "Crystal, there's something you're not telling me. What's wrong?"

"I'm just not doing well, and I want 'ou to pray for me."

There was no way I could get her to say any more about her problems. We had talked at times about how she believed God was going to do something more with her life, that she would be healed, and would not always be in an institution. So right then as we talked on the phone, I prayed for her: "Lord, You know how much I love Crystal. Thank You for bringing her into my life. I ask right now that You heal her. Lord, I beg You, give her my legs. You know my heart; I can take the wheelchair. Give her my legs so she can walk—"

Crystal interrupted me: "Harol', I don't want 'our legs."

"But Crystal—"

"The wheelchair is my pulpit, Harol'. It's my ministry. I am freer in this wheelchair than most people who have complete use of their bodies. I don't have 'egs, but I've 'ot Jesuh. And He's all I need."

That night I knew I'd witnessed genuine faith. Here was a woman who had never experienced the love of her parents, never climbed a tree or peddled a bicycle, and never known the love of a man. But she knew the love of God. Crystal knew God could heal her instantly with a snap of His fingers; she also knew her wheelchair would then be empty. She wasn't jumping out of her wheelchair because she didn't believe God enough, but because God wanted to use her right where she was. She was doing more for Jesus in her condition than most of us who are completely healthy. Yes, Crystal had true faith that could move mountains, and she'd learned it through suffering.

By exercising tough faith, Crystal had moved beyond her barriers. She was more free, despite her physical handicap, than I ever was when I received my parole. Her example was further motivation to go back to Georgia State Penitentiary to fulfill a twelve-year-old dream.

Chapter Twelve

THE HOMECOMING

There are certain events so firmly implanted in my memory that years later I can relive them in vivid detail. Receiving news that the governor of Georgia had issued me a pardon was one of those events. Lying in a hospital bed, hearing the doctor report I had cancer was another, as was the day I first met Michael Godwin. These three experiences seem like they happened yesterday. My day with Crystal and Mary Sue will certainly be a similar memory in future years.

Another memorable day was Christmas 1974, less than a year after my conversion. Christmas was always the low point of the year while I was in prison. Even as a Christian, I felt trapped in a bare cell with nothing but the memories of what I was missing at home. There was no Christmas tree, no smells of roast turkey and pecan pie coming from mother's kitchen, no family with whom I could share presents and meaningful conversation. In prison, Christmas was just like any other day, except the guards sometimes handed out a tiny Christmas packet, consisting of a couple of new razor blades and a few pieces of stale candy. We also had a special dinner, which included tossed green salad.

Many people would not consider tossed salad a special treat, but we had it only twice a year—on Thanksgiving and Christmas. It was such a big deal that inmates piled it high on their plates, as if there was an unlimited supply. There wasn't. When I finally reached the serving table on that particular day, the salad bowl was empty.

It was bad enough enduring the loneliness of prison on Christmas day. But I was disgusted that a few inmates took all they wanted, and the rest of us got nothing. In frustration, I picked up the huge metal salad bowl and drop-kicked it against the far wall. A hush came over the dining room as the bowl clattered and rolled around on the floor. "Someday after I'm released, I'm coming back here to give everybody a real Christmas!" I bellowed. The inmates and guards roared with laughter. A man with two life sentences dies in prison; he doesn't get out and then return as Santa Claus.

I never forgot that pledge. And in the fall of 1986, I shared it for the first time with four Atlanta businessmen: Bubba Cathy, son of S. Truett Cathy, the founder of Chick-Fil-A; Chip Murray, a banker; Al Cain, a successful realtor; and Danny Benson, a land developer. We were meeting at the headquarters of Chick-Fil-A, a company I'd long respected for its Christian business practices and the fact that none of its 350 restaurants were open Sundays. I told the men about my dream to give the inmates at Georgia State Penitentiary a bag of Christmas presents that they would remember and use for weeks. Many of the men hadn't received even a letter, much less a gift, for years. This would be a tangible way to show them God's love.

With the support and enthusiasm of these four friends, we began making contacts to see what could be donated or purchased at cost. By December first, each of our one thousand shopping bags contained a towel, a pair of socks, a box of raisins, a tube of toothpaste and a toothbrush, deodorant, several bags of candy, three kinds of peanuts, potato chips, Fritos, a package of chewing gum, a pen and tablet of writing paper, a bottle of Pepsi, a copy of my book *Twice Pardoned*, a slice of apple pie and a wallet-sized card good for one free Chick-Fil-A sandwich. That last item was my favorite; on the bottom was stamped: "Expires December, 2025." I knew many of the inmates with long sentences would hoot about that.

I also assembled a group of nineteen volunteers, including my old friends Bobby Richardson, Bob Norris, and Clebe McClary to help distribute the bags, since we'd only have three hours to complete the task. A few people questioned my sanity. "Who's paying for this?" one man asked.

"I don't know yet," I responded. "Some of the gifts were donated, and we've had a few financial contributions. What's not covered I'll pay for myself."

The man just shook his head. Obviously he thought the whole idea was a waste of time and resources. He didn't view these inmates as desperate souls who were lonely and forgotten during this most special time of the year.

To me, the gift bags represented a significant outreach. If the inmates thought about it, they'd have to ask why an ex-con would return to prison with gifts for one thousand otherwise forgotten men. Ultimately, I wanted them to realize that these gifts were from Jesus. That was why I included my book among the gifts. When they saw who the author was, many would stay up all night reading it. They would read about how I discovered Jesus Christ while lying in that same roach-infested prison. I wanted them to become like me, not in the sense of who I was as a man, but as a Christian loved by a personal God who promised never to leave us or forsake us.

As the big event drew near, I received a letter from Bull Jackson. In it he wrote his Christmas wish list: "I wants to get out of prison and move into the country. I'd builds me a house and a carport, because I's a good carpenter. And I'd grows me a little garden with tomatoes and anything else I wants. And when I's not taking care of my house and garden, I'd use my spare time to do a little carpentry and brick work to earns me some money."

Bull said he was reading the Bible I'd sent him. "But it ain't easy," he wrote, "because they gots a bunch of young guys in here doin' dope, and they's don't understand me. Prison ain't like it used to be. Everybody has changed."

I had to laugh. Everybody had changed, *including* Bull Jackson. I thought about his desperate plea a few months earlier, his desire to get out of prison after forty-two years and to smell the roses one more time. He knew that probably wouldn't happen. But the one thing he couldn't bear was the prospect of a burial in the prison cemetery, with nothing more than a number for his memory. I would have some good news for him when we met this time.

On December 6, Chip Murray and I loaded the bags on a truck provided by Chick-Fil-A and drove it two hundred-plus miles to the penitentiary. It was a cloudy, cold day as we arrived and unloaded at a warehouse on the compound. I couldn't help comparing the scene with my memorable visit five months earlier when I'd seen Bull Jackson come to Christ. The main prison building seemed more foreboding, and the chain link fence and razor wire looked even more threatening. But there was a warm feeling inside, knowing that this year the men would have something to cheer their spirits and provide hope even though they remained behind these formidable physical barriers.

The guards counted and inspected the bags. The only item they asked us to remove was the chewing gum; some industrious inmate might use it to cover up his work if he was trying to saw through the bars of his cell.

Chip and I drove the empty truck back to Atlanta, and the next day all of the volunteers flew from Atlanta to Reidsville, seven miles from the penitentiary. The warden arranged to have us picked up in two of the prison vans. It was a fitting welcome, because each was built like a penitentiary with no knobs or handles inside, and heavy bars and wire mesh separating the passengers' and driver's compartments.

In contrast to my earlier summer visit, we all were quickly admitted and processed. In the rotunda of the main building, we divided into three groups. One group was about to follow me until one of the guards motioned for me to go with him onto the elevator. That meant I was heading for solitary confinement and the hospital.

Without the volunteers around, I noticed again the oppressive sounds, smells, and sights of prison. After exiting the elevator, we passed through two gates, and as they shut behind me with a jarring clang and reverberation, memories of my years here were resurrected. I had to force myself to think not of the past but about my mission, and the joy and hope these men could find in spite of their harsh surroundings.

I visited those in protective custody first. These were men waiting to be tried by the internal prison court, or who were locked away from the main population because they were a threat to the other inmates. Their floor consisted of a dark hall with a long row of cells down each side. A guard followed me with a laundry basket containing the Christmas bags. I walked up to the first cell and announced, "Santa Claus is here!" A young man, probably not more than twenty-one years old, scrambled off his bunk and took the bag. "Merry Christmas! I love you!" I told him.

The boy had a dazed expression on his face and for a moment he stood in his cell just holding the bag. He seemed unsure what to do. Then he turned the bag over and dumped the contents on his bed. Quickly he spread all the goods out, then picked up the book and stared at my picture on the cover.

"You wrote this?" he grunted.

I nodded. "It's about where you're living and sleeping," I answered. "I lived here for seven of my nearly ten years in prison. I wanted to come back and let you know that I love you, and hopefully make your Christmas a little happier."

The young man seemed in shock. Reverently he put the book down, walked over to the bars, and offered his hand. "Thank you," he said quietly as we shook hands.

One black man, built like a truck, was opposite the first cell I visited. He watched me go up one side of the cell block, and then back down the other. When I finally handed him his bag, all he could do was stare at me. He was unable to say anything. As I grasped his hand and wished him a Merry Christmas, a single tear trickled down his cheek.

From protective custody, I took the elevator up to the hospital unit. After handing out several bags, I suddenly noticed Bull. I almost didn't recognize him. His ankles and wrists were swollen like bad fruit, and he looked feeble. I was shocked at how much he had deteriorated in the five months since I'd seen him. It seemed hard to believe that this man was the most feared inmate in the institution. Even more surprising was the mellow look I saw in his face. It was especially noticeable in his eyes; they no longer glowed with that inner rage that had driven him for so many years.

"Harold!" Bull said, greeting me with a wide grin. When I handed Bull his gift bag, he stared at it for a moment before saying, "This be the first Christmas present I's got in twelve years."

"I have something else for you," I said. "If you aren't released before you die, Chip Murray and I have made arrangements for your body to be turned over to us for a proper burial."

A look of pure relief passed over his face. "Harold, I's can't tells you what that means. You kept your promise. And even if I's don't gets to smell the roses one more time, at least I's won't be in prison after I's die."

Bull wanted me to stay and talk, but there was much work to do. He asked me to wait a minute as he shuffled to the back of his cell. After rummaging around for a moment, he returned with a broken pair of eyeglasses, reached through the bars and put them in my shirt pocket. "The lens is cracked, but they's won't fix my glasses. Do you thinks you's can get them fixed?"

"Sure, Bull. I'll do anything I can for you. Anything."

Unfortunately the guard saw the exchange, and as I moved on to the rest of the cells, he asked for the glasses. "You know better than that," he gently chided. "Nothing leaves the prison."

Reluctantly, I handed the glasses to the officer. I'd wanted to take care of that small need for Bull. I couldn't escape the fact that but for the grace of God, I'd been in the same spot. Instead of nearly ten years, I could have spent forty-plus years behind bars and died here, as Bull undoubtedly would.

The next two hours were among the happiest of my life. At every cell I announced, "Santa Claus is here!" as I continued handing out the gift bags.

One inmate was wearing an old pair of ragged long johns. The seat was torn out, one leg was ripped, and he wore no shirt. "Gosh, you didn't have to dress up for me," I said, handing him a sack through the bars.

One gray-haired man, after dumping the gifts on his bed, immediately picked up the Aqua-Fresh toothpaste in a pump container. "Just what I need—deodorant!" he said. As he started to squirt it into his armpit, I had to stop laughing long enough to tell him it was toothpaste. Toothpaste wasn't packaged in pumps before he went to prison.

Another man took the bag of peanuts provided by Delta Airlines, tore off the top, and poured the entire contents into his mouth. Then sounding just like a TV pitchman, he looked at the bag and commented, "Delta is my airline!"

After giving a bag to a young black man in his twenties, I walked on to the next cell. A moment later, the man called me back. "Stay out of trouble," he warned with what he thought was valuable advice. "Prison is no place to live." He hadn't seen my book, and didn't realize I'd lived in the same prison far longer than he had.

I spent a few extra minutes with a man to whom I'd earlier sent a Bible. He proudly waved it in front of me as I approached. "I've been reading my Bible," he said.

"Every day?" I asked.

"Yup!"

"What's your favorite book in the Bible?"

"Philadelphians!" he said proudly. "I like that cuz it talks about this guy, Paul, who was a jailbird, too!"

I also spent extra time with one inmate whose face was blotched with deep, bloody gouges. All over his unshirted torso were dozens of scars. Tattooed across the knuckles of one hand were the letters H-A-T-E. Across the other were the letters L-O-V-E. On each arm, he had tattooed MOM. He immediately took the three bags of peanuts—one salted, another unsalted, and a third honey roasted—and started stuffing them into his mouth. Perhaps he figured that if he didn't eat them immediately, they'd be stolen. I waited as he chewed and chewed. Finally, I asked him why his face and body were all scratched up. At first he didn't answer. "Did you do it yourself?" I asked.

He shrugged. "I put most of them there, but a lot of other people put them there, too."

"Why would you hurt yourself?"

"Sometimes I go crazy. I want to kill a guard or an inmate; I want to hurt them bad. But when I can't get to them, I get myself."

"You're going to kill yourself."

"Yeah, maybe," he said with a shrug.

What a tragedy, I thought as I continued passing out the gifts. I wished I could have had more time to talk, but I'd have to postpone that for another trip. In the meantime, I prayed that the inmate would read my book and come to know Jesus Christ—the only One able to remove the hate that was destroying him.

At the end of the day, after all of the bags were distributed, the volunteers assembled in the rotunda before departing. As we were about to load up the vans, Clebe McClary handed me a note which an inmate had slipped to him earlier in the day. The name on it nearly took my breath away. Randy Adams. I hadn't seen him in sixteen years.

I went straight to the warden and said, "Everybody's got to wait. I must go back and see this man."

A deputy warden escorted Chip Murray and me back to the prison block.

"You know how old Randy was when I first met him?" I asked. "Fourteen. I was in the county jail, and they put him in there with all the murderers, thieves, rapists, and drug addicts. I tried to protect him."

"He's in pretty bad shape," the deputy said.

Finally, at the end of a long hallway, the deputy stopped and unlocked a cell door. Inside was a man who looked weathered. He took a good look at me, and then hobbled over and threw his arms around my neck.

"I knew it was you!" he said in a voice choked with emotion. "I just knew it was you! If you only knew how many times I've thought of you and wondered what happened to you. After all these years . . ." he said, his voice trailing off.

"Randy Adams," I said, holding him at arm's length. "Let me get a good look at you." The last time I'd seen him he was a pimple-faced fourteen-year-old kid. Sixteen years later, his face was prematurely wrinkled and covered with scars, and there were streaks of gray through his tangled mop of mud-brown hair.

Randy was about six-foot-two, and skinny as one of the bars on his cell door. Every exposed part of his body had gash marks. Some had healed, others had festered. On his bony wrists were slash marks, obviously recent. He looked filthy, and smelled like old hamburger.

I asked the deputy if we could meet privately, and he ushered us into a nearby holding room just outside the cell block, locking Chip and me in with Randy. During our short walk, I noticed that Randy hobbled badly on his right foot and dragged his left leg. I asked what the problem was.

"Leg's been amputated just below the hip," he answered.

"How about your right foot, what's wrong with it?"

"Part of my toes are missing."

As I sat looking at him, I remembered him as a scared kid acting tough in the county jail. It was a terrifying place for a youngster, and I tried to help him. But he wouldn't listen to my advice. One night in a fit of anger, he'd stabbed me with a fountain pen. But most of the time he respected me, and I became his protector. I didn't see him again after I was shipped to Georgia State Penitentiary. "Randy, tell me what's happened in your life since we were together," I said.

"Got raped right after you were transferred," he said. "Wanted to kill the sorry convict, but then I got released. That was all right, being out again, but it didn't last long. I got nailed in Florida for stealing a car. Then I robbed a bank and did time in a Florida state pen for several years. Got released again and came back to Georgia, but they busted me for drugs and . . . well, here I am. The guards, they've shot me four times trying to escape. Now I got diabetes and am going blind. They don't give me long to live."

"Randy, how about the slash marks?" I asked.

"I put some of them there. Others were from fights."

"What about your throat?" I asked, eyeballing the expansive purple mark that cut from one side of his neck to the other.

"Tried to kill myself. I just couldn't take it anymore. But I lived." Then he looked over at my friend and asked his name.

"Chip Murray."

"Mr. Murray," Randy said, pointing at me, "that man right there, I saw him take an iron pipe one time and beat a man almost to death because he was messing with me. Grabbed that pipe and went after him. Harold looked after me; protected me when anybody bothered me." I felt a twinge of embarrassment as Randy spoke. This was a side of my life that I didn't want resurrected.

Looking at Randy, I felt a lump in my throat. He had a man's body, what was left of it, but in his eyes I saw a scared fourteen-year-old boy who'd never grown up. He was a shell of a man, the perfect picture of a wasted life. If the warden had told me to take Randy home with me, I couldn't have. Randy simply could not have survived on the outside. What could a man do who was missing his left leg and part of his right foot, who was going blind, and was popping all kinds of pills to medicate the last months of his life? Without insurance, who would pay the medical bills? What company would hire him? Where would he live?

But escape was all Randy could think about. "Harold, you got to help me get out of here," he suddenly pleaded. "I don't want to die here. I ain't got long to live, you see. I'd try to go over the fence, but they've already shot me four times. And now I can't even run."

I nodded without saying anything. It was tragic, but I realized that Randy was better off in prison, though I couldn't tell him that. I didn't know what to say. His eyes studied my face before he finally broke the silence. "Harold, I don't understand. You used to hate God. I heard you cuss God when we were in prison. You said there was no God. I remember that."

"Yeah, Randy, I remember that, too," I said.

"But you come here, and you do something no one has ever done. You give us stuff. You write a book about God helping you. I don't understand. Tell me something. Did God really do all this? Did He really help you?"

"Yes, Randy, He did. Let me tell you what happened." I briefly told him the story of my life, and about how Clebe McClary visited me in prison and led me to the Lord. "Isn't this something," I said. "The man God used to change my life is the same man who walked up to your cell today and handed you my book. That isn't a coincidence, Randy. Think about it!"

"God really changed your life, didn't He? If you can change, I guess anybody can."

"That's right, Randy, anybody can. Let me tell you how to know Christ. You've first got to realize you are sinner. You know I'm a sinner, because you've just told Chip things about me that I'm ashamed of, things that most people don't know about my past. But just like you know I'm a sinner, you also need to admit the same thing about yourself. You just told me you use drugs, that you've stolen other people's cars and money. God wants something better for your life, and Jesus died for you so that you could have it. That's what it means to be a Christian. It's realizing that Jesus died for you. You've got to believe that."

"I believe that, Harold."

"And you've got to believe He took your place when He died, and that His blood covered the penalty for your sin."

"Yes, I believe that, too."

"Becoming a Christian is the simplest thing in the world. It's by faith that you receive Christ. You can't see Him, you can't feel Him. But if you trust Him and receive Him, He will come into your life, change it, and use you in the lives of other people. God uses people, Randy, and He can use you, too. I will get you a Bible. I will come back. I will help you take a stand for Christ. Your life will never be the same. But first you've got to pray and invite Christ into your heart. Would you like to do that?"

"I'll do anything you want."

"No, Randy. Don't do it for me. I know this is an emotional time. But *you* must want to change. You must give Christ a chance to work in your life and help you. I can't save you, is that clear? I would like to take you out of here today and change you, but I can't do it. Only Christ can."

"I understand that," he said, yearningly. "I want Christ more than anything."

"Okay, then, I am going to pray. If it applies to you, repeat the words after me." I prayed aloud, and Randy repeated every word after me: "Lord Jesus, I recognize I am a sinner and that

You died for me on the cross. I want to receive You into my heart. Please take away my sins, cleanse me, and change my life. Help me to not cut myself up, to quit drugs, alcohol, and cigarettes. I want You to give me the courage to take a stand here and be a witness for You."

When we said "Amen," Randy threw his arms around me. I could feel the desperation in his fingers as they dug into my shoulders, and he didn't let go for a very long time.

The results of our Christmas visit were better than anything I could have thought in my wildest imaginations. As we drove to a motel for the night, one of my friends handed me a note from an inmate he'd visited. The note was brief and to the point: "Harold, thanks for the Christmas gifts. In Christian love, Shotgun Kelly."

I couldn't believe it. In *Christian* love? It was written plain as day by a man who'd killed at least three people. Shotgun Kelly a Christian? He was the neighbor who'd snarled to me my first day on death row, "Hey, next door, I'm going to kill you." Somehow in the intervening years, some inmate or visitor had told Shotgun about the Lord. The same man who had once vowed to kill me was now a brother in Christ.

My amazement didn't stop there. A week after our visit, I received a thank-you card signed by 190 inmates. Others wrote individual letters to say that my book gave them new hope. Some of the Christians wrote to tell me how the Lord was using their lives behind bars. Of course, there were a few con artists who wrote to say they were innocent, too, and asked me to speak to their judge, or call their parents, or help them find a job.

The most precious letter was from Randy. "It's four o'clock in the morning, and I just finished reading your book," he wrote. "You will never know what your visit has meant in my life. God sent you here, and now I am saved. But I am not going to live long, and I know it. Before I die, I'd just ask one favor. I've got a fourteen-year-old nephew who doesn't live far from you. He is on drugs, and is going down the same path that led me to prison.

"Please, Harold, don't let him become what I am. He's the

same age I was when I got into trouble. The last sixteen years, I've been outside prison less than one year. I don't want anybody to have to repeat my life, but I'm afraid he might if something doesn't happen to change things. My family has disowned me, and they'd never let me speak to him. Please, Harold, help my nephew. Tell him about me—how I ruined my life. And tell him about Jesus."

As I read Randy's letter, I was heartened to see a man who, in his first day as a young believer, wanted to reach out and help somebody else. Though his own life was wasted and almost over, he had a burden for another person who was following in his footsteps toward disaster.

We continued to correspond, and I sent him a little money, a Bible, and some Bible study guides. One day Randy wrote: "Harold, you'd be proud of me. I haven't smoked a cigarette for two days, and I never thought I could quit." His next letter reported: "Harold, I'm sorry, but I started smoking again. I'm weak." It was followed by another several weeks later: "Harold, I went a week without a smoke this time. I am going to give cigarettes up yet. I'm going to lick them. You told me I could do it, and I know the Lord is helping me. I used to smoke three packs a day, but I'm going to quit for good."

I was pleased that Randy was trying to give up cigarettes. I didn't tell him to give up anything. But I did tell him he had to fight sin, and that as he drew closer to God he'd want to change. That's how I knew Randy was saved. He *desired* to change. He recognized that he was a new creature. The old things were passed away, and all things became new. But the battle was continuous. He said that he was having a hard time because the homosexual inmates were hounding him. "I don't want to hurt anybody, Harold," he said. "Please pray for me."

I thought often about Randy, and how, in a sense, his life represented my work. He was a vivid picture of the toll that alcohol, drugs, and wrong choices can have on a teenager who follows the wrong crowd. In one letter, Randy wrote: "I wish I could do what you are doing. I wish I could tell young people that drugs kill. I wish they could see my body, all chopped up and scarred, because then they might understand. My life has just been a very long, slow, painful process of dying."

What a tragedy. And yet at the same time, Randy also demonstrated that there are no hopeless cases. No matter what a person's condition, the work of Jesus Christ guaranteed that change was possible. God could take a life, no matter how warped or useless, and produce something of incredible value. There were *no* insurmountable barriers.

That was the lesson of my life, and in the years God had allowed me to work for Him, I could see many examples of tough faith overcoming great obstacles. Hebrews 11, a chapter in the Bible sometimes known as the Hall of Faith, contained the names of people, including Abraham, Isaac, Jacob, Joseph, and Moses. They and others were all recognized for their faith, even though they didn't see all of God's promises fulfilled in their lifetimes. I could add to that list some of my own candidates; people who had demonstrated great faith to me.

I thought of little Toby whose mother had deserted him. His tough faith was willing to keep praying for her in the hopes that one day she would love him and love God.

I thought of Becky whose heart was broken by the sudden death of her husband and son. Tough faith enabled her to work through her grief, raise a beautiful daughter, and then reach out to others who were hurting.

I thought of Sasha at Southeastern Bible College who wouldn't let her family background and financial hardships prevent her from obeying God's call to the mission field.

I thought of Cynthia whose mistake caused her to drop out of high school and have a baby. But through tough faith she faced her problem, rejected the route of abortion, returned to school, and helped other girls going through similar struggles.

I thought of Michael Godwin who overcame his miserable childhood and raging hostility, and decided instead to use his God-given intellect. Rather than destroying people with his fists, he was saving them with his bold proclamation of the Gospel.

I thought of Linda O'Malley, fighting for her life in a battle with cancer. Her tough faith overcame her bitterness toward God, and accepted the fact that to live is Christ, and to die is gain.

Finally, I thought of Crystal Lavelle, a woman who had endured every human disadvantage possible. Rejected by her parents, disabled by cerebral palsy, confined in an institution, her tough faith refused to accept that her life was useless. As a result, literally thousands of lives have been touched by her prayers and witness.

All of these were ordinary people living extraordinary lives because they took God's truth, claimed it as their own, and practiced it in difficult, even tragic, circumstances. That's what tough faith is all about. Bull Jackson and Randy Adams were two new trophies of God's grace. It might be late, but they could exercise tough faith, too.

All around me were many more Tobys, Beckys, Cynthias, Michaels, Lindas and Crystals. As long as God allowed me to live, I could have joy in reaching out and knowing and being enriched by their faith. Through God's grace, I might even be the human instrument that sparks the faith in their lives.

But why should I be the only one so enriched? All of us can exercise tough faith. All of us have people around us who are hurting; people whom we can reach out and help. All that is required is our availability. And then God will open our eyes, enabling us to *see* those around us who need our love. Tough faith will then respond, helping these people move beyond their own barriers.